MUSIC & POLITICS

MUSIC & POLITICS

by John Sinclair
and Robert Levin

The World Publishing Company
New York and Cleveland

Published by The World Publishing Company
Published simultaneously in Canada
by Nelson, Foster & Scott Ltd.
First printing—1971
Copyright © 1965, 1967, 1969, 1970, 1971
by Jazz & Pop
All rights reserved
Library of Congress catalog card number: 72-149584
Printed in the United States of America

WORLD PUBLISHING
TIMES MIRROR

Contents

FOREWORD

Music & Politics is composed of articles, reviews, interviews, polemics, and manifestos—many of them very controversial, none of them less than provocative—which poet-revolutionary John Sinclair and essayist-poet-playwright Robert Levin have published in *Jazz & Pop* magazine. Although these pieces were not written with the expectancy that they would become chapters of a book, we think that together in one volume they make up what is very much a *book*, not just a "collection." All of the pieces are directly related and connected, not only by their subject matter—the extramusical, political, and social aspects and significance of rock and the New Black Music—but by a bold and abiding revolutionary vision which, each in his way, Sinclair and Levin share, and which inspires, shapes, and unites everything they write about the New Music. (John, chairman of the White Panther party, sent his work from a cell in Marquette Prison, where he is currently serving a *9½- to 10-year* sentence for his political persuasion—the "official" indictment said "possession of two marijuana cigarettes.")

I'm very proud to be associated with this book. I think it has valuable things to say about the myriad ways in which rock and the New Black Music, and the musicians involved in these phenomena, are reflecting and influencing our complex contemporary culture.

Pauline Rivelli, Publisher, JAZZ & POP

ABBREVIATIONS

Where the personnel and song titles of record albums are listed, the following instrumental abbreviations are used:

as—alto saxophone
b—bass
b cl—bass clarinet
bs—baritone saxophone
c—cornet
cl—clarinet
d—drums

f—flute
flh—flugelhorn
frh—French horn
g—guitar
o—oboe
or—organ
p—piano

ss—soprano saxophone
tb—trombone
tp—trumpet
ts—tenor saxophone
tu—tuba
vb—vibraphone
vo—vocalist

JOHN SINCLAIR

1970

A Review of
Chick Corea's *Is**

I love the music on this record—it's some of the freest and
most alive music to be heard today. I had never really *heard*
Chick Corea's playing before, or dug the scope of his music,
until I had the opportunity to listen to this record at some
length (courtesy of the Michigan penal system). I have seen
his name and heard his playing as a sideman, you know, for
some years, but I had never really *thought* of Chick Corea, if
you know what I mean, and I wasn't at all excited about this
album until I put it on the machine and got under my head-
phones. But once this music is heard, it's a whole different
thing, or at least it was for me, and Chick Corea is a name
now that passes through my head sometimes, all day long, and
I love to get back to my cell after a long day in the prison
laundry and put this record *Is* on the box and get into it
for a long time while I write home on my typewriter. This
is some high-energy music, and these brothers really kick out
the jams, as we used to say in Detroit.

*CHICK COREA. *Is* (Solid State SS18055): Chick Corea (p); Dave Holland
(b); Jack DeJohnette (d); Hubert Laws (f, piccolo); Woody Shaw (tp);
Horace Arnold (d); unidentified tenor saxophonist. *Is; Jamala; This; It.*

Chick Corea, Dave Holland (who plays some killer electric bass, as well as acoustic on this album), and Jack De-Johnette are now Miles Davis' partners, as people probably know already, and from the reports I read in the papers, they do this stuff on stage with Miles and Wayne (Shorter) all the time. I had heard them on *Filles de Kilimanjaro*, which is a *quiet* high-energy jam, if you can relate to that, but that's nothing like the music they make here except in spirit. The spirit is the same, the inspiration is the same, the breathing; it's just the manifestation of that spirit which is different here—the music is faster and friskier and even freer, which is where it's at finally. And instead of Miles and Wayne, the three regulars are joined by (and with) Hubert Laws, flute and piccolo, and Woody Shaw, trumpet, and an unidentified tenor saxophonist. And the liner notes says that there's another drummer named Horace Arnold on the record, but I can't tell from the equipment I have—this Montgomery Ward Airline special—whether there are two drummers on this record or not. I don't know anything about Horace Arnold, I haven't even heard his name before, but I'm wondering if he might not be the tenor player and if it isn't just DeJohnette who's kicking up all that excitement on drums? It may be that Arnold is playing along with DeJohnette and I just can't distinguish the second set of drums from the first due to my box being inadequate—but I'm not complaining. I'm happy to have the use of it; after all (to paraphrase an old cliché about people in Europe who are starving), there are brothers in B-Block who don't get to listen to record players at all.

I'm not complaining, is all I'm trying to say. It's hard to complain with this beautiful music charging through my head right now. I wish I could tell you who this tenor player is, because he is smoking over Dave Holland's Fender bass right this minute, but you will have to find out who he is some other way, if you must know. Sometimes I can almost put my finger on who he is, but then I can't finally, and

4

that's not really the issue anyway. We really do get carried away a lot with all the Hollywood consciousness of the music industry and tend to concern ourselves—I know I have seen this tendency in myself and in other people too—with personalities and S*T*A*R*s and personnel and dates and shit like that, as against the import and inspiration of the music itself, but we have to remember—*always*—that it's the music, the *music* and the *lives* of the musicians *and* the people, the musicians *as* the people and not as something glittery and separate *from* the people, not the individual consciousness but the whole spirit of the people that makes this high life and high art, this high human culture of ours possible, that gives us sustenance and life and charges our flesh and our spirit with life. All that other shit is just a ruse. So, brother tenor player, I wish I could tell these people who you are so they would know to buy your records in the future, and bring you in a few cents' royalties so you could eat and sleep and work a little better, but you and I know, and the people know too, I think, that the music you make on this record with Chick Corea carries its own weight, and will bring you its own reward someday too, if it hasn't already. Right on, then.*

Woody Shaw is the trumpet player, there's no doubt about that, and Chick Corea plays plenty piano. Hubert Laws makes it too; actually, he contributes considerable color and light to the music, puts a top on it, and he works very closely with the tenor player to create some high-charged lines and flurries. On *Jamala* especially they work together to build a spiraling line out of nothing, out of a whisper from Corea's piano, that develops into a crazy whirling hurricane propelled faster and faster by DeJohnette and Dave Holland. Maybe there *are* two drummers on this record—the percussion work sure is strong—but it seems to me that Jack DeJohnette is capable of taking care of all that business himself; I know he can do it, there's no doubt in my mind about

---

*The saxophone player has been identified as Benny Maupin.

that; I just wonder if he's got some help here or not. But that's not the point either.

It's hard to tell about drummers anymore—there are so many drummers now who can play so much more drums than anyone has ever played before, and Jack DeJohnette is certainly one of them, along with Elvin Jones, of course, and Tony Williams, and Andrew Cyrille, and Rashied Ali, and the always dangerous Sunny Murray, "secret hero of these poems," along with Steve McCall and Thurman Barker and Phillip Wilson of Chicago, and I have to say Danny Spencer and Bud Pangler in Detroit, Everett Brown, Jr., in Los Angeles, and there are some rock-and-roll drummers who can do it too, but Ginger Baker isn't one of them. Mitch Mitchell is, and Keith Moon; and Dennis Thompson can do it when they let him (which ain't too much anymore); and Scott Bailey of the Up will play like that too when he gets his growth; and there are probably a number of other brothers I should talk about, but I can't. George Brown and Billy Hart, I can't forget you, though. And Jack DeJohnette on this record by Chick Corea, and if there is a drummer named Horace Arnold and he is playing on this record like it says there, then the two of them epitomize *modern* drumming, and define it, and if you listen to this record, maybe all of this will make sense. But that's only as it should be.

So on this record *Jamala* starts out in a whisper and rises and rises and shouts and hollers and gets it on *completely*, and *This* is a sweet kind of tune that stretches out into something else altogether and slips back into its original premise at the end, and there's a pause, and then it almost repeats itself for the 27 seconds of *It*. And you turn the record over, and on the other side *Is* is a 29-minute free-for-all that reminds me of home so bad I can *feel* it just like I was there. This is *free* music, music that's free to develop, move, shift, grow, change, and flow with the feelings and breathings of its makers; and these brothers really do let it flow. People, "readers" is what I meant to say, who are into the rock/dope scene can relate to this music better maybe if I say that this is genuine *head* music, *trip* music, music that's much farther out than anything being produced by the pop industry, even Frank Zappa (is that a blasphemy?), or even the Pink Floyd and people like that when they used to be far out. I haven't heard what the Pink Floyd are doing currently, their smash-hit album on Harvest Records, *Ummagumma*, but I see in the papers that they are getting special nights at the Fillmore and big ads everywhere you look. And the music on this record by Chick Corea & friends is much farther out than anything you will hear there, and it's better *for* you too.

I'm sorry to say that I haven't seen *any* ads for this record *Is* by Chick Corea, and I don't see Chick Corea and Co. playing any nights at the Fillmore, and they don't seem to be on the hip "progressive-rock" (Isn't that like "progressive jazz"? What ever happened to Stan Kenton?) stations, and even the hip-hip underground pop writers seem to have missed this release, so maybe it isn't what it sounds like to me. Because it sounds plenty hip to these ears. And I'm wondering if maybe TransAmerica Corporation, which owns Solid State, might not start hyping its really far-out releases like this one (and they shouldn't forget Blue Note, and the Cecil Taylor records they have there, and Don Cherry, and Ornette, and Andrew Hill, and on and on) in the same way they push their big pop hits—maybe if this big monster Moloch merchandising machine TransAmerica would start pushing its "jazz" music and musicians to the pop audience, the people out there in music-market-land would start to get a little bit of what they deserve from the record companies instead of just the same low-energy bullshit they're stuck with now. The people can't buy and can't listen to what they don't know exists, and it seems funny that the record companies don't ever bother to try to expose their jazz and new-music players and performers to the mass audience. The people will certainly relate to it if it is presented properly, and the people deserve the best there is. And I have to say—I'm happy to say—that this record *Is* by Chick Corea rates with the best music available right now or any time. Keep it up, brother Corea, brother Holland, brother DeJohnette, keep it up, and I will keep hoping that the people can someday get to where you are, waiting for them, with all that music.

1970

A Review of Marion Brown's *Le Temps Fou**

If there is a new music scene, or a new-music scene—and
I have to refer to the music still as *new* music, or new-music,
now some ten or twelve or fifteen years since it first emerged,
or started to emerge, in all its various shapes and feelings,
because it is still *new*, it is still best characterized by that
term, it is still newer and fresher and more vital than any
other music or musics to be heard, and you should know
that I am not one bit unfamiliar with the whole of the
pop/rock business and its products—if there *is* a new-music
scene on this planet, it must be in Europe now, where this
record of Marion's was recorded and released, and where so
many of our free musicians have gone to work and perform
for real audiences. They have not gone there by choice—
although many brothers have found out that Europe *is* a whole

*MARION BROWN. *Le Temps Fou* (Polydor [France] 658-142): Marion
Brown (as, bells); Gunter Hampel (vb, b cl, tree bells); Ambrose Jackson
(tp, cow bells, tambourine); Barre Phillips (b, castanets, whistle); Steve
McCall (d, triangle, tambourine); Alain Corneau (claves, cow bells).
*Le Temps Fou; Cascatelles; Song for Serge and Helle; Boat Rock; Yé
Yé; En Arrière.* (Recorded in Paris as the soundtrack for the Marcel Camus
film *Le Temps Fou.*)

different living experience than Raceland, USA, that the level of official violence perpetrated by the consumer-capitalist society on its people is far lower and far less intense at all times there—but because they have been almost systematically excluded from the remunerative music business in this country, and likewise from any possibility of an audience. These musicians, who are men who love their country and their own people, who would be happy indeed to have the chance to work and perform for their people here in their native land, these musicians who in many cases have worked hard and long to try to create new working and performing conditions for their music and their people, so the people will have freer access to the music in its freest and purest manifestations, these musicians have been forced to move to Europe in order to get an audience and enough remuneration to enable them to continue their work.

I know I shouldn't bother you with all of this just to review this record of some of Marion Brown's recent work in music, but you will never hear this record anyway, and the reason you won't hear it is precisely because it isn't available in this country, just as the musicians aren't available here anymore, although I understand that Marion is back in the USA now with a new wife, or I should say, a newly married wife, back in Atlanta, Georgia, but that doesn't bring his music any closer to you, since there is no place you can go to hear him, no record companies or booking agents hunting him down to sign him to contracts, put out records of his music, bring him to the Fillmore or Carnegie Hall or Madison Square Garden; you dig, none of this is happening, and this record has not even been released here. Which is par for the course, to use a peculiarly American metaphor, in these last days of the Amerikan empire. I mean that Richard Nixon has not asked Marion Brown and Gunter Hampel and Steve McCall to come to the White House and play *Boat Rock*, or *Welfare Cadillac*, or whatever, for the various animals assembled there, and he never will.

A Review of Marion Brown's Le Temps Fou

We have to deal with these things when we talk about
music, because the people are being denied even the opportunity to hear music of this nature, music of this intense
human nature, and it is no longer possible for me just to
talk about the music as if it were something independent and
unconnected with the life of the people. We don't get to
hear the music we need, and we suffer for all that, even
though most of us aren't even aware of that lack in our lives
—we don't get to hear the music we need, and our heroic
musicians suffer even more than we do for this lack. Because
there is not much life for a musician without an audience—
especially when the musician is as committed as these musicians are to the full expression of the world/spirit that
charges through their bodies, to the full communication of
that spirit/feeling through their music to the people, to the
people's bodies and lives, to as many people as can be con-
vinced or persuaded or harangued into listening to and taking
in this beautiful music.

This music is a people's music finally, and the musicians
are sick with the separation of the music from the people.
I don't want to pose as any kind of maudlin spokesman for
these musicians—they can speak very eloquently, and very
beautifully and precisely, for themselves, and they do that
in their music too—but you should all know about this long-
ing, by these musicians, for your attention. They make this
music for you, not because they want you to "buy" it, to
"own" the records and contribute to the GNP—although that
wouldn't hurt so much insofar as the musicians would be
given that much more little security to eat and sleep and
work without scraping and hustling and shit; they make this
music for you because the people, you people, are the natural
term of this music, Can you dig that? Joseph Jarman, another brilliant brother who is in Europe now after fleeing
Pig City (Chicago), where he recorded two of the most
beautiful records you will ever hear—Jarman wrote on his
second album. *As If It Were the Seasons,* "we sing because/

we love you/because we/love you/because/we love/you"—
you dig? The music is for the people, and the people are
a first term of the music, just as the instruments and the
notes and sounds and the players are a first term. There is
no separation, except as the ugly consumer economy inserts
itself between the musicians and the people and dictates just
who will get to relate to the people and who will not.

So you hear the latest whimper from England or Scars-
dale, the latest rumored pop genius who once played back-up
guitar for Phil Spector, or who sucked off Bob Dylan's dog
one night at the Café Wha in Greenwich Village, or who
used to shine shoes in front of the office building where the
Beatles and the Rolling Stones met Allen Klein, or who was
discovered by Bill Graham shooting speed under the chair
in the dressing room of the Fillmore East while Delaney &
Bonnie & all their Heavy Friends (as in Lord Sutch) were
performing weird obscene acts on each other's toenails on
stage. You hear all these people as soon as their managers
and agents and record companies and promotion firms and
sideburns and underground columnists and body shirts and
shit can get their drivel before your ears and eyes. But men
—MUSICIANS—artists and workers of the stature of Marion Brown and Joseph Jarman, Roscoe Mitchell and Don
Cherry, of the absolute genius stature of Archie Shepp, Pharaoh Sanders, Albert Ayler, Cecil Taylor, dynamite genius
brothers whose music will knock you absolutely on your ass
once you hear it—Sun Ra, the Jazz Composers Guild Orchestra, whew!—are still wandering around New York City and
Amerika and Europe looking for a few people to listen to
them, for a few hundred brothers and sisters who will let
this music pass through their bodies on its way to completion, pass through their bodies and open them up to the
new energy universes this music bears witness to, testifies to
and uncovers with every breath and phrase.

I can't really deal with that whole problem here, though,
of how the music business has, I almost have to say, *con-*

spired, to deny these men and this music the opportunity to meet and inform its proper listeners. For the purpose of this short review, I will have to say only that this record by Marion Brown is not available in the United States, it has not been released here, you won't hear it on the radio, you won't see Marion on TV, but one day you may have the chance to hear and feel this man's music, and you will be happy when you do. But now you will not be able to hear *Boat Rock* off this record, or the space music of *En Arrière* or *Le Temps Fou* or *Cascatelles* or *Yé Yé*, which you would like very much if you could hear it. There are some of Marion's works available here, though, and I would refer you to his Impulse album *Three for Archie, Three for Me,* particularly *Spooks* and the tunes with Stanley Cowell playing piano on them; and I would refer you to Archie Shepp's record *Fire Music,* and a song called *Hambone* where Marion plays his guts out, his heart out, and a song called *Taking It Out of the Ground* on a Burton Green album (ESP 1024) where Marion and a tenor saxophonist named Frank Smith will tear your head open, or to Marion's solo on John Coltrane's album masterpiece *Ascension,* you dig, where Marion scalds out a killer solo that will make you jump and shout; or to Marion's own ESP album, the beautiful pulsing music there, *Exhibition, 23 Cooper Square,* and the other side I can't remember the name of, with Alan Shorter and Benny Maupin and Rashied Ali and Reggie Johnson—you can get this music here in Amerika, and you really should. You will love Marion's music, when you hear it, just as it loves you even now.

Motor City Music

These two records* have been available for some months now, but since no one seems to know about them, I thought I'd try to pull some people's coats to these two manifestations of stomp-down Midwestern rock-and-roll music. The Rationals and the SRC have been together, as working (performing) bands, for a long time now, especially as rock-and-roll bands go, but their activity has been confined primarily to the Detroit-Ann Arbor-Midwestern scene, which is another phenomenon I want to talk about here in order to put their music in its proper context.

The Rats started out as a high-school teen-rock band in

*THE RATIONALS. (CGC 1334): Scott Morgan (vo, p, percussion, or, g); Steve Correll (g, vo, percussion); Terry Trabandt (b, vo, p); Bill Figg (d, vb, percussion). *Barefootin'; Temptation's 'Bout to Get Me; Guitar Army; Something's Got a Hold on Me; Deep Red; Sunset; Glowin'; Handbags and Glad Rags; Ha-Ha.*

SRC. *Traveller's Tale* (Capitol SKAO-273); Scott Richardson (lead vo); Glenn Quakenbush (or, p, vo); Al Wilmot (b, vo); E.G. Clawson (d, vo). *A New Crusader; Street Without a Name; Midnight Fever; Never Before Now; By Way of You; Diana; Across the Land of Light; The Offering.*

their hometown of Ann Arbor and had some local 45 hits as far back as 1965. Their biggest Michigan smash, a good version of *Respect* taken from Otis Redding before Aretha Franklin got her beautiful throat around it, took them to a short-lived recording contract (45's only) with Cameo-Parkway Records, if that gives you some idea of their roots. That is to say, they were recording locally some time before most of the current wave of Detroit-Ann Arbor bands was doing anything more than playing the local high-school dances and teen clubs—although Mitch Ryder was sockin' out the jams then, as he is now with his new band called, very precisely, Detroit, and Bob Seger, who's made some of the best singles in rock-and-roll history—*Heavy Music, East Side Story, Ramblin' Gamblin' Man, 2 + 2 Is on My Mind*—was just starting to record, but the Rationals were right there with them, in front, playing the big disc-jockey hops and state-fair gigs and high-school dances which were the only outlets for the music and the rock-and-roll teenagers of the time.

The SRC has its roots in two classic Detroit bands, the Chosen Few (who with the MC-5 opened the Grande Ballroom in October, 1966) and the Fugitives, who did some local recording on the Hideout label and played mostly at a string of weird teen clubs run by Punch Andrews and Dave Leone (now of DMA Management/Booking in Detroit) and called the Hideouts—they were really K of C halls and places like that which these dudes would rent out on Friday or Saturday nights for 150 dollars and pack the kids in to hear and *dance to* the Fugitives, the Rats, Bob Seger and the Last Heard, the MC-5, and bands like that. Scott Richardson, who sang lead with the Chosen Few (their bass player, Ron Asheton, now plays guitar with the Stooges), got together with the remnants of the disbanded Fugitives (minus their piano player, one Boot Hill, who then joined a great Detroit blues band called Billy C. and the Sunshine [Billy C. now sings and plays harp with Commander Cody and his New Lost Planet Airmen] and later played with Sam

Lay's Mojoworkers and then with one of Mitch Ryder's recent Detroit bands) and formed the Scott Richard Case early in 1967. They recorded a single of *I'm So Glad* (the Cream arrangement off the first Cream LP) which hit big in Michigan on the A^2 label, then changed their name to SRC and signed with Capitol to do three albums, of which *Traveller's Tale* is the latest and the greatest. The Rationals' album, on the other hand, is their first, although they were supposed to sign with Capitol at one time, but the deal fell through.

That's a fast superficial history of these two bands, but it doesn't really say anything about their very real development as local forces in the Detroit-Ann Arbor rock-and-roll culture, which is something not very many people outside of Michigan know anything about. There are reasons for that, and they all have to do with the greater context of the American pop scene, which is controlled not by the people or the bands but by a handful of huge record companies and their agents, paid and unpaid, in the public-relations industry and the pop press, and another handful of club owners and concert festival promoters who book their "acts" according to the styles and trends invented by the record companies and their flacks (and if that sounds too strained, check the bookings at the Fillmore East sometime and tell me which bands don't have record contracts with which labels).

But just because it was never "discovered" (as, say, Columbus "discovered" America) by the industry doesn't mean that there wasn't a tremendous concentration of rock-and-roll energy and talent in Detroit. The Motor City scene, as it existed at its height in 1968–69, was the strongest and also the farthest-out rock-and-roll center in the world, even though the bands and the people who were involved in it didn't have any idea of how strong and beautiful their thing was. Having been brought up in the plastic morass of America and taught that only the "experts" (the ones with the big money) know what's happening at any given time and place, the bands and the people in Detroit had (and still have) the feeling that their scene wasn't shit because they weren't reading about it all the time in the papers, or watching it on TV, no big-shot pop fashion-mongers were dribbling out their precious opinions about Detroit music (although we did manage to sucker some people into coming out to hear the MC-5 in 1968—it scared them to death and they never came back). The record companies were reluctant to come out too, and when we did get some attention with the MC-5 and the Stooges, *Time* magazine called it a "revolutionary hype" and *Rolling Stone* followed suit, so the owners weren't too eager to risk anything more on that kind of situation.

The sorry thing is that by the time the Detroit-Ann Arbor scene reached its maturity as a hotbed of rock-and-roll music and culture, and was due to be "discovered" by the industry as such, localism as a force in the pop world was dead. It had flourished briefly (and I'm talking about the market sense, not the sense of immediate utility to the people of a particular area, although that comes in too) in San Francisco-Berkeley in 1966–67, during which period the Detroit scene was just starting to come together, but it was over by the next year—the rock-and-roll imperialists had moved in to buy up all the music and energy in San Francisco, and, seeing their success, MGM then tried to *invent* a local commercial gold mine for themselves (the infamous "Bosstown Sound" hype built on the shaky ground of Orpheus and the Beacon Street Union), and that killed off localism altogether. The pop writers and taste-makers were afraid to say anything rash about any new local phenomenon because, having little sense of the *music* in itself, they were afraid they'd be as embarrassed as those people were who fell for MGM's rancid bait in Boston.

But there was—and believe it, there still is—a strong, indigenous rock-and-roll scene happening in Detroit at that time, a scene which was peculiar to Detroit and which was important for just that reason: because music and musicians are important in the widest sense, as they reflect and likewise shape the consciousness of the people out of whom they emerge to make the music. And the most important—that is to say, the most *useful* —are those which reflect and shape the purest and highest (energy) stages of people's consciousness, *i.e.*, revolutionary consciousness. The Detroit music scene was and is built on the consciousness of the people of the youth colony there, and it was and is shaped precisely by the social circumstances which surround it and give life to it. In other words, this music couldn't have emerged anywhere else, nor at any time other than that out of which it did emerge, and since it was so precise to its roots, it has had an equally precise effect on the people who gave rise to it, which is the highest use to which music can put itself.

Now, the SRC and the Rationals are and always have been integral forces in the Detroit scene—they have been defined by it and they have likewise helped very much to define it. The purest manifestation of what I mean by the Detroit sound was the MC-5 in its prime, 1968–69, which coincided with the prime of the scene too, and in order to understand what that scene was all about, it would be worth some time to talk about the 5 and their music. When they were *doing it*, the MC-5 were the most explosive musical force—at least within the context of rock-and-roll music—on the planet, and they were also the most *contemporary* rock-and-roll group in existence, contemporary in the sense that they made full use of the contemporary possibilities for rock-and-roll expression, possibilities which are being ignored or perverted now by almost every group on the (international) set. I mean the possibilities of amplification and power, electricity and energy, total feeling and total involvement on every level, especially audience involvement with the music on the highest and deepest level.

The MC-5 *were* a "whole thing," as I wrote at the time; they were one with the music and one with their people; there was no separation, and everybody got down together in the music, which gave expression to their collective consciousness in that time and place. The MC-5's music was wholly integrated—it was inspired by the people and the social conditions in Detroit, and in a purely musical term it was integrated on a different level, being based on the *sound* they built up out of their banks of amplifiers and speakers (something they were into long before the "big" groups started using all that equipment). Their songs were constructed out of that sound, to give definition to the sound and to the social circumstances out of which the sound was born. The power of the amplifiers was built into the songs and arrangements of other people's songs they used; they were not separable from it, and in that sense the MC-5 made what best can be described as "post-Western" music, in the same sense that Archie Shepp's or John Coltrane's or Cecil Taylor's or Sun Ra's music can only be called post-Western. That is, these musics destroy separation on every level, and separation is the basis of all Western musics up to and including most of rock-and-roll expression.

Now, the so-called "classical" or European music is the most blatant example of this phenomenon, where a "composer" writes out a "score" to be played somewhere else by a bunch of musicians who are given only to interpret the lollipops on the page handed them by the "conductor." The form of the music, or the score, is entirely separated from its content, or the musicians playing the score out. (This is also a perfect model, as all pure music is, of the social structure which produces the music, if you can dig that.) And all popular music in the West since the "great composers" of Europe is based on this essential separation of form from content, which reached its zenith (or nadir, is the way I'd have to put it) with the Broadway musical tunes of the thirties and forties and fifties. That is, the music itself can be characterized as inseparable from the social conditions which produced it, but the strictly musical basis of that phenomenon is the separation of the songs from the performer —*anybody* can sing *Blue Moon*, and make it mean *anything*, even Bob Dylan, who means less and less these days.

In the same way the Beatles' "greatest hits," to take only the most immediately available example, can be divorced or separated entirely from the fact of the Beatles' playing of them and be performed by string orchestras, by "jazz" players like Wes Montgomery or Bud Shank, or by other pop groups and singers with as much effect as the original version, simply because these songs are firmly in the Western musical-social tradition.

Bebop likewise is a Western music, since it proposes a definite form as separable from the possible content, a form which can be filled up with the content of any number of musicians who adhere to the rhythmic, harmonic, and/or melodic forms of a particular piece of music. Bebop players, like "classical" or any other Western musicians, don't even have to know one another to get together and play the music; all they have to do is accept the formal propositions of the music and do it more or less together, *i.e.*, at the same time and in the same place.

Most rock-and-roll music is "Western" in the same term, and I should make it clear that I'm not using "Western" as any kind of derogation really—I mean there is excellent Western music, moving Western music, etc., but the point is that it *is* Western music, and that's what I'm trying to deal with. Thus you have, in rock and roll, the phenomenon of bands playing other bands' tunes all the time, and you even have what existed in bebop circles in the middle fifties especially, the concept of all-star or session date recording, which extends increasingly into performance situations also. I mean Blind Faith (really!) or Delaney & Bonnie & Friends, or Crosby Stills Nash and Young (and it isn't any accident that that sounds like a law firm) are just an extension of Jazz at the Philharmonic, you dig, and Mike Bloomfield-Al Kooper-Steve Stills are just an extension of the Prestige and Blue Note Friday afternoon sessions of 1955–57, except there's a lot more money involved, and the music isn't as exciting. The musicians even shoot a lot of smack, like they used to do in the fifties, if you can relate to that. (See, for example, the section on Jackie McLean in A. B. Spellman's great book *Four Lives in the Bebop Business*.)

It was only natural, then, that the MC-5 related so strongly at one time to the music of Sun Ra, Archie Shepp, Trane, Pharaoh Sanders, et al., because they were to rock and roll what these brothers are to "jazz music"—its extension into the post-Western "present future" (LeRoi Jones's term). Their music, like that of these other brothers, grew directly out of their social stance, and defined and reflected that stance in musical form. And the music itself was inseparable from the *persona* of the musicians involved—they lived for the music, the music gave expression to their lives, they were one with it in equal term. The form of their music was inseparable from its content—the sound, the sense of the words of the songs, the lives of the musicians—and was wholly precise to those particular five musicians. In fact, it was Rob Tyner who first told me, one night when we were driving back from a teen-club gig somewhere, that *Separation Is Doom*, and it really is.

I spend so much time and space on the MC-5 here because they are absolutely germane to any discussion of Detroit music —they represented, in their prime, the purest expression of the general thrust of the Detroit *sound*, and they were instrumental in creating that sound and that scene too. The other major Detroit-Ann Arbor bands (with the exception of the mighty Up, who are even purer than the 5 ever were) embody that *sound* in varying degrees of purity, and their effect on the development of that *scene* has been felt in relation to the degree to which they embody the sound. All of them are more or less shaped by the peculiar circumstances of the Detroit-Ann Arbor scene, in the same way that (going back to where I jumped off from some time ago) all the San Francisco-Berkeley bands are reflective of the unique social conditions which obtained in the Bay Area when the music was emerging, and (to take it a step further) the whole body of Detroit music is a unique thing *as a whole*, the same way the whole body of San Francisco music is unique.

I'm not going to try to set up an exact analogy, but since most people who follow pop music are familiar with the San

Francisco bands, I'll take this a little further and draw some correspondences which may make the Detroit scene more accessible to you all, since you don't know much about *it* at all. In one term the MC-5, the Up, and possibly the Stooges are analogous to Jefferson Airplane, the Grateful Dead, and Big Brother and the Holding Company in its first prime, in that they represent the purest expression of what is meant by a Detroit sound, and also in that they reflect the general consciousness of *their* people. This doesn't have anything to do with their music as compared to the music of the analogous SF bands, but is meant only to suggest that as the Airplane, say, incorporates all of the elements active in the SF music as a whole, so did the MC-5 in its prime—and so does the Up now —incorporate all the elements active in the Detroit scene, and in their purest form.

The difference between the two cultural centers—Detroit and San Francisco—is evident in their music, as the music is always the purest formal expression of the social forces at work in any given scene; and where the SF scene is characterized by a "folk"-blues-based music, a low-pressure good-vibes feeling, and a loose freaky relationship with its audiences, the Detroit scene can equally be characterized by a rock- and urban-soul-based music, an intense high-energy feeling, and a close, tight involvement with *its* audience. And these qualities are also evident in the same term in the music of each place as they are evident in the physical and social life of the two metropolitan complexes.

I mean that San Francisco and Detroit are probably polar opposites in terms of the general social context of America today: San Francisco being the loosest, most open, freest metropolitan center in the country, existing, as it does, at the extreme western edge of Western civilization in its purest sense (which is only to say that Japan is not purely Western yet) and retaining some of the positive characteristics of the Western frontier; while Detroit, in the center of the country both physically and metaphorically, is one of the tightest, nastiest, dirtiest, most rigidly policed cities in Amerika. For a quick example, when the first be-ins emerged in all their glory in early 1967, San Francisco accepted them more or less warmly, since they were born out of the open social situation there and reflected that situation, albeit in its freakiest form; but when we organized a love-in in Detroit that same spring, in happy emulation of the San Francisco scene, the Detroit police rode down on the people there and ended up beating and clubbing hundreds of longhairs while chasing us out of the park we had begged from the city for the day.

When the summer of love was flowering in San Francisco that year, ten thousand people were arrested in Detroit as the inhabitants of the black and poor-white colonies rose up to strike out at the police and industrial oppression they felt every day. And the neighborhood where the freaks lived in Detroit was the center of the uprising, the physical center of the city, and the sector which bears the brunt of the constant police terrorism directed against the people. While the Airplane and the Dead were playing in the parks of San Francisco, the MC-5 and the UP were barricading their doors against police attacks and bailing each other out of jail. So like I say, the music came to reflect that social situation, and came to represent it as precisely as the Dead's acid flash reflected the SF scene.

I keep meaning to get back to where I started from with these two records by the Rationals and the SRC, but I have to give some sense of the context out of which they and their music have emerged, because nothing makes sense divorced from its context, and I want you to hear these records as the people out here in the Midwest hear them and as what they are in fact—a manifestation (or two manifestations) of a clearly defined cultural complex which is unique and which is precise to it social origins. I take so much time on this because there hasn't been until just now any coherent attempt made (and I'm not so sure *I'm* being coherent even now!) to deal with the Detroit-music phenomenon as what it is, the only fully developed *local* culture in America outside of San Francisco. See, the *local* is the only stick we have to beat universalism back with and reclaim our culture from the creeps who have ripped it off from us. Universalism, as in this description or dictum from LeRoi Jones's *Black Music:* "The New Music . . . is cooled off when it begins to reject blank, any place 'universal' humbug. It is this fag or that kook, and not the fire and promise and need for evolution into a higher species. The artist's resources must be of the strongest, purest possible caliber. They must be truest and straightest and deepest. Where is the deepest feeling in our lives? There is the deepest and most meaningful art and life. Beware the 'golden touch,' it will kill everything you useta [used to] love." You dig?

This *local* emerged as a force for change in this place, as I suggested above, with the maturation of the San Francisco scene in 1966–67, but as soon as it stuck its beautiful head out, it was snatched off and adulterated by the imperialist robber barons of the mother-country music industry, who took it to their manufacturing plants and packaged it and sent it out as a separable thing, divorced from its roots in the local scene it grew out of (SF music, I mean). By the time the San Francisco music scene matured, it was no longer a *San Francisco* (local) scene, it was a "universal" scene which could be bought at the nearest record counter and imitated anywhere records were sold. The *form* of the SF culture—its music most precisely, but also its posters, its clothing innovations, its chemical agents, even (or especially) its unique dance/concert forms—was separated from its *content* in the true Western capitalist tradition and packaged up as a great new American commodity for kids all over the world to buy up, who could then take it home wherever they were and use it up (consume it) without being touched really by its original (radical) content, that is, by the example of the lives of the musicians and the people who based their new lives on the music of those musicians.

Maybe I'm not being clear enough. Let me put it this way: what the record companies and the forces they represent are interested in from our culture is commodities which they can package and sell for a profit. The music means nothing to them, or means nothing unless it poses itself as a threat to their class hegemony by, for example, persuasively advocating the destruction of Western thought and the capitalist economic system. Then they will get interested, concerned enough at least to put this threat out of commission one way or the other, by denying it further access to the means of production which they control, or by buying it off, which for their purposes is even better. Since the overwhelming majority of the bands and people who get into the "rock business" through the music are incredibly naïve about the economic and social realities of this place, they are usually very easy to deal with from the point of view of the rock-and-roll imperialists; in fact, they are usually only too eager to do whatever is asked of them, and they will do it all in the name either of good vibes or of that good old Amerikan dollar.

When San Francisco people's culture started to flower in 1966–67, it was easy for the r-&-r imperialists to rip off its products because the musicians and the movers in the scene had such a beautifully beatific vision—they felt (and most of us at that time felt, or at least, I myself felt) that this was going to be the way to turn on the great American public to the new spirit/culture, by sending out the new spirit music through the established mass media. Recording contracts were eagerly sought and accepted, and soon all the bands who had any "commercial potential" were safely brought within the confines of the standard American economic form, that is, monopoly capitalism.

The bands accepted the terms of the music industry more or less unconsciously and started doing the things that were expected of them—making record after record, going on tour around the country, doing the Ed Sullivan Show, and everything else short of endorsing Wheaties or Breck Shampoo (which I'm sure they would've accepted equally if the opportunity had been offered them). Now, there's nothing wrong with doing this stuff in itself—the mass media and its adjuncts *can* be used to advance the interests of the people, *if* one is aware of the possibilities and the pitfalls involved and takes care to protect oneself against the corrupting influences which are built into these forms—but the way it happened, with the bands and other entertainers essentially unaware of the effects of their actions and of the negative effects of the media through which they were projecting themselves and their music, the bands soon lost their radical charge without even knowing it; and it's going to take some major changes for them to regain that charge.

I mean they were corrupted and robbed of their revolutionary potential simply through the process of gradual erosion and creeping decay. Since they weren't prepared to *resist* the corrosive effects of the consumer-commodity ruse, they were taken in by it in their innocence and were increasingly shaped by the plastic forms into which they were dumped by the r-&-r imperialists, if you can dig that. I mean, you don't travel across the country, cut off from your roots in the people, segregated from the people in plastic motels and fortresslike hotels, eating in honkoid restaurants, surrounded by industry hype men and deranged sex freaks, playing one night here and one weekend there, every week in a different place, for months, with your price and your isolation increasing all the time, without being affected by that process; one morning you wake up in Cincinnati, say, where you're playing in a baseball stadium at $10,000 for a forty-five-minute "live" version of your album hits and where your people are getting beat up by the police rented for the night, for your protection, by the greedhead promoters, you wake up in the morning in some weird hotel and you light up a joint and suddenly you realize that you aren't what you were when you started playing the music for people you knew and loved, you're something else altogether, and if you keep it up you know you'll be playing golf in Las Vegas in a year or two with Bob Hope and Spiro T. Agnew, checking out the stock-market reports to see how your investments are doing, and cursing the godless communists in Vietnam and South America and Ann Arbor who refuse to be subjected to the final obscenity of the consumer society you play such a large part in pushing.

Or have your lawyer issue a statement condemning record bootleggers who refuse to play the monopoly market game and instead tape your concerts and sell them directly to the people who dig the music—who do they think they *are*, anyway? Don't they know that this music is sacred and already belongs to Warner Brothers?—or you give interviews putting down the "irresponsible radicals" who are demanding that a number of people be let in to your concert free that night, or that you play for the benefit of Bobby Seale or Pun Plamondon or some other prisoners of war in Amerika. And while your price goes up to $25,000 and then $50,000 a night, you cry about how these "childish radicals" are "ruining the music business." You dig? You forget that you didn't used to have any money either, and that you started out playing your music for the people because you loved both of them equally—the music and the people—and that you had visions of a whole new life on the planet which just doesn't seem possible now, because, well, everybody just can't *have* a fine house in Marin County and chauffeur-driven limousine or an $18,000 Aston-Martin to drive to the bank in.

That's what I mean by the effect of the rock-and-roll imperialists and their consumer-market consciousness on the very form and content of the music, and how the "universalism" of the monopoly-capitalist economy destroys the potentially revolutionary effect and cause of the music. The *local* is discarded as a possibility for the culture because it just isn't profitable enough, and the only standard becomes that of the market, the money, and not the possible utility of the music at all. And the people get less and less important too, until they're reduced to the status of simple consumers, ciphers to be packed into hockey arenas or baseball stadiums or decrepit old racetracks at $15 a head, or ruined old movie theaters at a nickel ($5) or "3.50, 4.50, and 5.50" a seat. A *seat*, you dig, when everybody used to dance all over the place and really get it on together.

But dancing is out, because you can get more people into a place and keep them in line better when you make them sit down, and besides, all the high explosive energy gets drained out of the music, and you can't really dance to it anymore anyway, it's more like the Ed Sullivan Show, where the people just sit there and eat it all up, and then go home and shit it out and get more and more bored by the whole thing. The means of production move more and more into the hands of fewer and fewer owners, and the taste of money wipes out the taste of honey altogether.

"I don't want to scare you, but they mean to kill all of us," or something like that is what E. E. Cummings once wrote, and what that says here is that the greedheads mean to kill us all off as anything more than consumers of the culture we've created out of our own cells and visions as something which was meant to sustain us and give us more life. Now, all it's good for is to keep us in line (on the street or in front of the box office) and sustain the power-ego-greed drives of the "owners." Whew! And of course there's no more room in this scheme of things for a local, an indigenous, true-to-its-roots culture created by the people's bands and cultural workers for the people to give expression to the consciousness of the people—there's no room for it, it just ain't profitable, you know?

It's quaint and all, but we just can't use it, pal, let's be realistic, it just ain't what's happening anymore, and did you hear about the great new superfestival with Ten Years After, Led Zeppelin, Jethro Tull, the Black Dyke Mills Brass Band, the entire population of Northern Tibet, the Philadelphia Symphony Orchestra featuring Paul McCartney, Dave Brubeck with Maria Callas, and Rudolph Bing, the Ringling Bros. Circus, the entire Lincoln Park Zoo, and Bob Dylan's bar mitzvah reenacted by Al Kooper and Mike Bloomfield, with lights by the Department of Defense and sound equipment by Disneyland? Oh wow, man, it's just too much, and it's only $83.00 plus tax if you can dig it. And they're bringing in Alfred Hitchcock to film it, courtesy of Linda Eastman-Kodak, and the whole thing will be produced by, who else, Warner Brothers in cooperation with Gene Autry and Bob Hope. Wow!

O.K., what does all of this have to do with these two records by the SRC and the Rationals of Ann Arbor, Michigan? People, it has everything to do with them, because if you think about it for a while, you'll maybe start to realize that there are reasons why you have never heard of these bands or the music they produce out here in the middle of Amerika, where they play week after week for their brothers and sisters in teen clubs and obscure ballrooms which are not owned by Bill Graham, and summer resorts run by people who wish they were, and in the parks for free on Sunday afternoons. And if you check it out a little more, you might see that these two bands, and their brother bands out here, are part of a scene that is struggling to define itself as something different from the standardized plastic bullshit pop industry scene which is posited as the only possible answer to our need for music and life of our own making.

These bands are part of an alternative which is becoming more and more absolutely necessary for the survival of our culture, and the sad part of it is that they themselves would probably be happy to go along with the bullshit if they were only given the chance to get their hands in the great pie in the sky being dished out to the select few by the greedheads of the mother-country music industry. I can't say that these two bands are consciously revolutionary in their intent, but the effect is what counts finally, and their effect is considerable. Listen to the Rats sing *Guitar Army*, is what I mean to say. Or *A New Crusader*, by the SRC, which is precisely what we need right now. These bands, and their brother bands out here, have become a powerful force for change just because they *haven't* been "discovered" by the industry, and the scene they are part of will develop in its purest direction, finally, simply because it hasn't been certified by the pigs as the "happening thing, baby." And that's right on, too.

I keep wanting to say more about the music on these records, because it's excellent rock-and-roll music played and meant for high-energy rock-and-roll people, but I would really like to have you hear it for yourself if you will—you'll get a lot more out of it that way. The Rationals album is one of the most consistently satisfying rock-and-roll records I've ever heard, with a great selection of original songs and killer adaptations of rock-and-roll classics like *Temptation's 'Bout to Get Me*, Robert Parker's *Barefootin'*, *Glowin'* by the good Dr. John, and *Something's Got a Hold on Me*, that something being the music and the people, and, oh, it must be love.

Scott Morgan, who is one of the strongest singers and most versatile instrumentalists in all of rock and roll, has a voice that never lets up, and he uses it masterfully on everything he puts it to. He was offered the singing job with Blood, Sweat and Tears when Al Kooper left, but turned it down to stay with his brothers Steve Correll, Terry Trabandt, and Bill Figg at home in Ann Arbor; and David Clayton-Thomas was recruited to carry the message of "Amerikan youth" to the "Iron Curtain" countries for Dick and Spiro. That's all right too, because the people of Detroit and Ann Arbor are just that much better off, and if Scotty isn't salting away a large fortune, he's doing something that's a lot more useful, and which the people he plays for will be eternally thankful for once they realize what the deal is.

The SRC are an excellent rock-and-roll band too, and the only flaw in this album *Traveller's Tale* is the last song on it, a wimpy fantasy moan called *The Offering* which deserves only to be offed and *is* offed by the rest of the music on the record, particularly things like *Across the Land of Light* and *Midnight Fever* and *Diana* and *Never Before Now*. This music is hardcore representative Detroit-Ann Arbor music, and they're more powerful in person too. And their second album, called *Milestones* and also on Capitol records, has one of the finest rock-and-roll tunes I know on it, which is called *Up All Night* and which you should check out if you have a chance.

The Rats and the SRC are people's bands, bands which were born out of the indigenous culture of the Detroit-Ann Arbor rock-and-roll maniac scene. These are bands which are known and loved by the people they play for, bands which pick up and shape and reflect that people's feelings and dreams and aspirations with their every note, their every move on stage or in the streets of Ann Arbor, Michigan. There are a lot more bands like these out here where the rock-and-roll people still aren't aware of the cultural riches they have available to them, and there will be even more of them as our culture grows and flourishes on its own terms, nourished and inspired by the music and by the strength of the people's support. People out here are just beginning to realize finally that it is their own culture, their own bands, their own people who are most important to their own lives; and as this realization spreads, bands like the Rationals and the SRC—and the Up, the Brat, Brownsville Station, All the Lonely People, the Stooges, Mitch Ryder's Detroit, the Norman James Blues Band, Commander Cody and His New Lost Planet Airmen, the Frut, 3rd Power, Savage Grace, Frost, the Amboy Dukes, and even the MC-5 if they ever come back home—will be recognized as the tremendous forces they in fact are.

As I said earlier, music and musicians are important finally insofar as they reflect and shape the consciousness of the people out of which they emerged, and these two records are useful in that term as well as in a purely musical term. Music comes from the people and must return to the people; and the more directly, the better. We need a lot more bands like the Rationals and the SRC, and we need a lot more *local* scenes like the one they are part of. Universalism in music, as in everything else, must be beaten back by the local, and the control of the music must be returned to the people it comes from. Self-determination on all levels is what will save us and make us strong. Right on! All Power to the People! Power to Woodstock Nation! Long Live the People's Bands of Ann Arbor and Detroit! Long Live the People's Revolutionary Culture!

1970

Self-Determination Music*

What I would like to see is artists
owning as much of themselves as possible.
Or most people.

—George Russell, *Jazz & Pop*, April 1970

I really can't see much need for "reviewing" these records,

*The records under discussion in this piece include:
MAURICE MCINTYRE. *Humility in the Light of the Creator* (Delmark
419): Maurice McIntyre (ts, cl, bells, tambourine); Malachi Favors (b);
Mchaka Uba (b); Thurman Barker (d); Ajaramu (d); George Hines
(vo). *Suite: Ensemble Love (Kcab Emoh; Pluto Calling; Life Force;
Humility in the Light of the Creator)*. Hines out; add John Stubble-
field (ss); Claudine Myers (p); Leo Smith (tp, flh): *Suite: Ensemble
Fate (Family Tree; Say a Prayer For; Out There [If Anyone Should Call];
Melissa; Bishmillah)*.

SUN RA AND HIS ASTRO-INFINITY ARKESTRA. *Atlantis* (Saturn Research
507): Sun Ra (solar sound organ; solar sound instrument); John Gilmore
(ts, perc.); Bob Patrick (bs, fl); Marshall Allen (as, o); Danny Davis
(as); Danny Thompson (as, fl); Bob Barry (d, lightning drums); Wayne
Harris (tp); Ebah (tp); Carl Nimrod (space drums); James Jacson (log
drums); Robert Cummins (b cl); Ali Harsan (tb). *Mu; Lemuria; Yuca-
tan; Bimini; Atlantis*.

Self-Determination Music

SUN RA AND HIS ASTRO-INFINITY ARKESTRA. *Strange Strings* (Saturn Research 502): Sun Ra (electric piano, lightning drums, tympani); Thlan Aldridge (space voice); Clifford Jarvis (tympani, perc.); Marshall Allen (as, o); Pat Patrick (bs, fl); Danny Davis (as); Robert Cummins (b cl); Ali Harsan (tb); John Gilmore (ts); Ronnie Boykins (b) James Jacson (log drums). *Worlds Approaching; Strings Strange, Strange Strange.*

LIBERATION MUSIC ORCHESTRA. (Impulse 9183): Charlie Haden (b); Carla Bley (p); Mike Mantler (tp); Perry Robinson (cl); Gato Barbieri (ts, cl); Dewey Redman (as, ts); Don Cherry (co, fl); Sam Brown (g); Paul Motian (d). *The Introduction; Song of the United Front (El Quinto Regimiento, Los Cuatro Generales, Viva La Quince Brigada); The Ending to the First Side; Song for Che; War Orphans; The Interlude (Drinking Music);* add Andrew Cyrille (d): *Circus '68 '69; We Shall Overcome.*

HORACE TAPSCOTT QUINTET. *The Giant Is Awakened* (Flying Dutchman FDS 107): Horace Tapscott (p); Black Arthur Blythe (as); David Bryant (b); Walter Savage, Jr. (b); Everett Brown, Jr. (d). *The Giant Is Awakened; For Fats; The Dark Tree; Niger's Theme.*

STANLEY CROUCH. *Ain't No Ambulances fo No Nigguhs Tonight* (Flying Dutchman FDS 105): Stanley Crouch rapping and reading from his poetry and prose for the Black Students' Union in Los Angeles.

ELAINE BROWN. *Seize the Time* (Vault 131): Elaine Brown, voice, composer, with orchestra arranged and conducted by Horace Tapscott. *Seize the Time; The End of Silence; Very Black Man; Poppa's Come Home; Take It Away; The Panther; All Stood By; Assassination; The Meeting (Black Panther Party Anthem).*

A NIGHT AT SANTA RITA. (Flying Dutchman FDS 111): Rosko, recitation; James Spaulding (fl); Ron Carter (b); written by Robert Scheer.

SONNY SHARROCK. *Black Woman* (Vortex 2014): Sonny Sharrock (g); Linda Sharrock (vo); Dave Burrell (p); Norris Jones (b); Milford Graves (d): *Peanut.* Add Gary Sharrock (bells): *Black Woman.* Gary Sharrack out; add Teddy Daniel (tp); Richard Pierce (g): *Bialero; Blind Willy; Portrait of Linda in Three Colors, All Black.*

ROY AYERS. *Daddy Bug* (Atlantic 1528): Roy Ayers (v); Herbie Hancock (p); Buster Williams (b): Mickey Roker (d): *Daddy Bug; Bonita; Shadows; It Could Only Happen to You.* Ayers; Hancock; Ron Carter (b); Freddie Waits (d); *This Guy's in Love with You; I Love You Michelle; Look to the Sky.* Ayers; Sonny Sharrock (g); Hancock; Carter Bruno Carr (d): *Emmie.* String quartet on all selections conducted by Gene Orloff; woodwinds conducted by Jerome Richardson; produced by Herbie Mann.

at least not until enough people are listening to this music—these musics—that we can carry on an intelligent and knowledgeable discussion of the specific records, that is, until enough people are thoroughly *familiar* with the body of music, or musics, of which these records are part. *Familiar*, as in, *family*. So I have to see my task as creating or producing some effective *propaganda* for this music, or again, these musics, and these specific records, in the hopes that people can read what I write here and be moved somehow to procure copies of these records, take them home with them and introduce the music to their families, and let it become part of their lives. Because people are going to have to get to this music sooner or later, and the sooner the better—not only for the individual musicians and bands involved, but for the good of the whole people, if you can relate to that. Because this is liberation music, self-determination music, music that will help you, inspire you to transform yourself, yourselves, and to work to bring about the transformation of the social order which keeps so many of us, and so many more of our brothers and sisters, oppressed, hungry, and beaten down.

Now, I could talk about the music, but I want you to listen to it for yourselves, so I will restrict myself primarily to talking about the *context* in which the music is made, the extramusical aspects of the music (extramusical only in the sense that you will not be able to *hear* what I'm talking about here on the records when you listen to them, except as these things fully *inform* the music and make the music *possible*—you dig?). What I have to talk about is the human context of the music, then—the social and political realities which shape the music and which, equally, are shaped *by* the music. Because the music cannot be separated, must not be separated, except at the peril of the musicians and their audience and at the peril of the whole social order finally. The music may be strong in itself, it may hold, it may charge the listener, sure, but once the musician is separated from the music, once the music becomes less than the *first term* of his life (her life), once the listener becomes less than the first (equal) term of the music and the musicians equally, then what the people get is less than what they deserve, and there is something wrong with the whole situation, something wrong with the whole structure of that society in which the music is produced—it becomes, or comes to be, less than what it was *meant* to be, if you can relate to that.

Because music is the thing that gives us breath and strength, that sustains us and keeps us alive, and we live for the music, it lives and breathes for us, and when something else happens in there, when something disrupts the flow of the music through the musicians to the people, when those relations (*that* relation, really) are disrupted or corrupted, then the people are being cheated, and the musicians are being cheated, and the natural balance of the life of the people is destroyed. As it is so much today anyway, which is what we are trying to put a stop to now, which is what this music and these words, and the musicians' lives and our lives too, are dedicated and committed to stopping, this destruction of the balance of our lives. And what I want to say is that we have to start with the first things, the primary things, like our breath, our daily acts and gestures, and we have to integrate ourselves with the universe from our cells on out; we can't separate ourselves from our words, acts, or gestures, or from our music, or we are doomed. It has to start there, inside the skin, and the relations have to be maintained all the way out, through whatever other bodies or things that come into our lives.

Because if we are going to talk about liberation, we have to talk about liberation in the total sense, and we have to see that (1) there is no freedom that does not start at the root to grow out free—or you can't talk about being free, or sing about being free, without *being* free, and without manifesting that freedom *throughout* your activity equally; and (2) one person can't be free until all people are free. We have to learn these things as we can, because we are quite purposefully taught differently, but what is important is that we *are* learning, and the music is helping us learn about freedom. Liberation music, self-determination music, the two terms are coterminous, they define each other—and they help us define ourselves, as the music does. This music is meant to liberate you, just as it liberates the musicians as they play it, just as their own personal and collective liberation is the productive force of the music itself —these are free musicians, and they can make free music, and they can get this music to you to help you free yourselves so you can join with them then to help free the rest of the people.

Now, as we have been taught by other liberation fighters, we cannot deal with personal or cultural freedom without talking about and dealing with economic freedom, or the people's control of the means of production. And that's what makes these records even more interesting for me than many others which I could have written about—because all of the records under "review" here are products of economic self-determination programs as well as musical self-determination programs, and they are unique in this quality, or almost unique, by which qualification I mean only to say that there are other people putting out their own records too, or building their own self-determination programs, but these records here are truly exemplary, and must be seen as such. We can learn a lot from these records, not only from the music, but from the whole setting of the music, from the musicians' lives, and from their economic and productive relations.

Both of these conditions are instructive. The musicians' lives and their economic work (not just their musical work) have much which is of use to us in all we do. Because we have to change this world, and it is most important for us that we learn *how* to move—i.e., *how* to do that which we know must be done, that which *we ourselves* must do. And we can learn that from these men, we can learn varying approaches to the problem of self-determination for the artist and for all people— from the way in which Herbie Mann, an individual artist who is probably more interested in his own welfare than in wide social issues, has created his own production company so he can produce and market recordings of his (and Roy Ayers' in this instance) and retain maximum control over the ultimate product; to the *whole thing* that Sun Ra has made of his original impulse for musical creation, the way he has kept a band together for twenty years, has produced his own records, has kept full control of the music and everything associated with it in the hands of himself and his musicians, and all of this without even the most minimal remunerative consideration!

There is a whole range of activity demonstrated and manifested in these records, and these musics and musicians, but all of it just amounts to the barest beginning of the way of the future, which must and will be characterized by self-determination for all people and all activity on every level.

These men are the harbingers, some of the most beautiful and persuasive harbingers, of the New Order, and their activity points a way for all of us to explore. They have solved, or have at least begun to solve, the problem of separation—of the musicians' separation from the music, of the music's separation from the people it is meant for, of the musicians' separation from the means of production. One of the most beautiful things about this music—as exemplified by these albums—is the way the music is so close to the lives of the musicians, so close that it *can't* really be separated, so close that it can help destroy separation everywhere. Stanley Crouch says it best in his killer liner notes for the Horace Tapscott album:

> But the most important thing to understand is that these men are as new as this music, their lives and their music are not separate. They don't, like so many others, stop being warm as soon as they get from behind their instruments, don't rein up all the strength and knowledge they play with some cracker style shuck corny super hip "attitude" off the band stand. And that's the message, as Walter Lowe would say, "A way to live." Or as Horace says: "The relationship between you and me as men is the first thing, the piano is something else: I just use it for certain things."

Right on, Horace.

But that's not all of it, either—there's one more thing I have to get in here, and that is that the music, as the musicians' lives, is *revolutionary* music, music of the highest and most positive CHANGE effect—it is the highest energy music, the freeest, the most natural, the most *inspirational* music there is— not just these records, I mean, but the music or musics of which these recordings are just a small and representative part: because we have to talk about Cecil Taylor, we have to talk about Pharaoh Sanders, we have to talk about Albert Ayler and Archie Shepp and Joseph Jarman and Roscoe Mitchell and Marion Brown and Sunny Murray certainly, we have to talk about Richard Abrams and Alice Coltrane and Charles Moore and Gato Barbieri and Gunter Hampel, we have to talk about the Jazz Composers Orchestra, we have to talk about the whole range and scope of this music (these musics), and we have to see that the whole thing is more than just the music, we have to talk about self-determination for all peoples, we have to talk about the Black Panther party, and the National Liberation Front of South Vietnam and the People's Republic of China, and the Cuban Living Revolution, and the rising Youth Nation in Amerika and throughout the postindustrial world, we have to talk about the incredible force of high-energy rock and roll, we have to talk about the killer blues that gave birth to these musics in this land, we have to talk about oppressed people and their total human liberation, we have to talk about what Stanley Crouch says. "Human closeness, Natural Intimacy, the Natural Closeness of Human Beings, the Spiritual Principle beyond machines and madness is what playing [*like this*] teaches you, is what listening [*to this music*] to learn will let you know. . . . You can learn from the music because it's there to teach you, to put everybody close to himself or herself and every other self worth being close to"—which is *all selves,* when you get down to it. We have to deal with *everything* in its natural context and destroy separation on *every* level, and what I am trying to say is that this music—and I am *not* claiming too much for it—this music will drive us to do that if we let it.

Yes it will. *There is no separation,* unless we will it, or

38

unless it is forced on us, and if we will give our will and spirit over to Sun Ra, say, or Maurice McIntyre, or some of these other brothers and sisters, they will take care of us, they will breathe into us, inspire us, that is, and make us whole again, make us whole with our own selves and with the rest of our people. I mean, the music won't do it all, there is a life's work ahead of all of us, and we had better make ourselves aware of all that, but the music here will give us a start if we let it, and it will keep us going too, no matter what our privations, it will keep us committed to our struggle and inspire us certainly in our work, and will show us the way. I said once, "MUSIC IS REVOLUTION," but we have to *live* the music, we have to make *use* of it, we have to take it as inspiration and live *up* to it, give back what it gives us, take the charge of the music and transform it into action, just as the musicians transform that original breath-charge into music and give that music to us to use.

This is revolutionary music, then; it is what we need for our transformation; and our transformation is what is needed to remake the world we live in. But the music is only revolutionary as long as we make it that, as long as we let it move us to action, as long as we let it transform us from consumers to *makers*, as long as we don't just suck up all the energy in the music and keep it all in and just shit it out, like a consumer does, because this music is good only as long as it is used and converted into other forms of energy—if you try to swallow it all and keep it down, hold on to it, hoard it, use it for yourself only, it will only make you sick, and you won't be able to stand it at all. And in that case, you'd better go back to what you were listening to before, some kind of straight consumer shit that is made for the money only, made to glut you, made for you to consume and use up fast and shit out so you can buy some more as soon as the benevolent "owners" put some out on the market for you to buy. Leave this music alone, then; you know it won't do you any good at all, and you won't even like it, it's not being played at Bill Graham's clip joints, the palaces of Hollywood culture and the big entertainment buck, as they say; it's not being hyped by the hip-hip record companies, the underground dee-jays aren't playing it, the pop-magazine writers aren't hip to it, John Lennon's never heard of it, Bob Dylan's not to be bothered with it, Paul McCartney's wifey doesn't have a yen for it, it isn't sweeping the pop underground as the latest sensation, it's not being packaged and sold like it would have to be to be hip; and it's a whole other thing, you can't shuck and jive with this music, this is music that has a life of its own above and beyond any record contracts and booking agencies and gigs at the Filmore and stories in *Cosmopolitan* and *The New York Times,* you dig, even though this music and its musicians would accept and use all of those opportunities to reach the masses, but it is not limited by that *industry* consciousness, this is music that exists for itself, for its makers and for all the people, not in any order but all-three-at-once, and unlike Blind Faith or Ginger Baker's Air Force or the latest super-groovey new ex-John Mayall superstar band straight from England to Wall Street, these musicians will still be playing after the press parties and the first big American tours and the super-duper pop festivals and the $10,000-a-night gigs have been shoved into oblivion; these musicians are not going to be at each other's throats or in each other's pockets; they are not going to "break up" their music or their bands because the gigs are running out and the stories are getting fewer and farther between and the booking agents aren't as interested as they were and Bill Graham won't take them back unless they will accept third billing or some shit like that. This is music that exists because it *has* to exist, because the people need it, because the musicians need in their cells to make it, to make the *music* and not the whole Hollywood pop S*T*A*R scene. And you can't separate that whole reality from the records I've listed here, because that's one of the things that make them so beautiful, and so strong. I don't like especially to talk of these musics in terms of some other (more popular) musics and Muzaks, but in this context, since this is a "pop" magazine now and since we have to have some common frame of reference if we're going to talk about this shit, I have to do it this way. And I have to tell you that I know about the "pop" business, have taken part in it, know the possibilities and limitations of that scene inside and out, and it is an ugly fucking scene based on greed and exploitation on all levels, even though (as is usually the case in exploitative situations) the people who are producing the music, the raw labor force, aren't yet aware of what's happening to them. They're swept up in the phony glamour and amphetamine excitement of the whole S*T*A*R scene and don't realize that they're being bled for everything that they're worth, being bled and sucked dry and used against their own people at the same time, which is the ugliest part of the whole picture. Self-determination is not what's happening on the pop scene, except in the most harmless sense—harmless to the controllers, that is, not to the people who are managed by it—in which certain artists are given the power to determine the shape of their own records and performances and the power to rake in a bigger percentage of the bread for themselves to use to buy their Rolls Royces and Victorian mansions and shit like they're supposed to do. They stay entirely within the mold that's been made for them by the "owners," the avaricious pigs who run the music industry, and what freedom they're given is theirs only so long as they use it against their people, that is, as opposed to the humanistic end of stirring up the youth and black masses and leading them in striking down the rule of the "owners," moving the people to change themselves from consumers into total life-actors, to change themselves and the conditions in which they live and work and buy buy buy, to deal once and for all with the "ownership" class which controls and manipulates the music industry and the mass communications industry and the munitions and death industry and the educational industry and the whole industry of consumer society that is all tied inextricably together under corporate capitalism today.

I'll get back to that, but I want to make sure I'm clear on a couple of things first. There are two major questions here, and I want to make sure I keep the distinction clear: there is the contradiction between the freedom of the music and the anti-freedom of the conditions in which it is made, packaged, and sold; and there is the contradiction between musics (and musicians) which are free on all levels, which are born of freedom, and which breathe freedom into their listeners, and those musics which are not free in that term no matter how "freely" they are created or produced, those musics whose real productive life ends in the recording studio, whose musicians separate themselves from the music they create and send forth into the world. A lot of "pop" music, including some of the most powerful rock-and-roll music, however strong it is and however freely produced and controlled by its makers, is still not free in the total sense that I am concerned with in this essay, that is, its freedom *as music* does not extend to the whole context out of which it is made, the musicians' lives and actions which are previous to and go beyond the music itself.

The Rolling Stones is the best example I can think of. Now, their music is so beautiful sometimes, and some of it (*Sympathy for the Devil,* or *Street Fightin' Man,* or *Jumpin' Jack Flash,* for openers) is so powerful, but they are not and cannot rightly be called "free" musicians, because prior to and beyond the act of the music itself we are led back into their totally bourgeois lives, the uses to which they *put* their music (to make the big buck), their money (to consume conspicuously and to make more money only), and their lives (of utter luxury). They could be using themselves and their capital to deal with the needs of the people—there are bands and musicians on a much much lower economic level who do that, who put themselves entirely at the service of the people—but the Stones are satisfied to remain wholly in the bourgeois camp, and that has to be dealt with.

Now, this is something that pisses a lot of people off, but I have to deal with it, because it is absolutely central to the records here, to the music and the musicians under discussion here as well as to my own life and work. I know people don't like to hear this too much, but it is a fact that the artist has a greater responsibility to his people than just making his art available to them at a price. He, and she, has the responsibility of using all the advantages which accrue to the artist in this weirdo economic system, for the benefit of all the people—and especially in our culture, in the new youth culture which exists and struggles for new life in the belly of the monster white beast of consumer capitalism, in the bowels of the imperialist beast itself, in the stinking caskets of the death culture, especially in our Youth-Life culture where the musicians and popular entertainers have the only access our people get to the mass information media, and they have the only access we get to the capital which is needed in a capitalist society to fund self-determination programs for our people, especially in this situation is it important that the artists of our culture start using their personal advantages for the benefit of their people, which is finally for the benefit of all people, just because this monster beast is the perpetrator and guarantor of slavery all over the world, from South America to South Vietnam and Cambodia and Laos, from Watts to Washington, D.C.

These musicians and popular performers of our culture, these powerful brothers and sisters who can reach millions of people every time they open their mouths, these young geniuses who have millions of dollars at their command, are going to have to start relating to the problems of their people and putting themselves and their powers at the disposal of their people —they are going to have to relate to the people's needs and they are going to have to start leading the people toward self-determination on all levels. Now, I'm not putting them down, because I realize and I know that most of them don't know yet that this is what they have to do, and that's why I'm trying to get all of this down, so people might be able to relate to it this way, but what I'm saying is that they have to deal with this problem, they have to start relating to their people and start putting themselves wholly in the service of their people, or else they are finally no more than what? Than Lawrence Welk, or Pat Boone, you dig, or Spiro T. Agnew finally. Bob Hope. Or else they are just pigs like the rest of their fellow entertainers, pigs and class traitors and deniers of the people, and their music will be no more than the force which will inspire the people to rise up against them and destroy them along with the rest of the exploiters and perverters of the people.

O.K., I had to get that in there, and like I say, I know a lot of people will be pissed off when they read this, especially some of the musicians of our culture who don't like to be bothered with awful things like "politics" and prison sentences and the people's needs and problems and unpleasant things like that. They are meditating and counting their money and watching themselves on television in the back seats of their limousines, and they don't want to hear about this mundane shit—it messes up the good vibes, don't you know? Why, we have to play these tremendous rock operas and shit, we're playing at Philharmonic Hall or on the IT&T Hour on interstellar television, this is the most important shit in the Western world, man, and we don't wanna hear about Bobby Seale and the Vietnamese peasants and power to the people and all that stuff. Tim Leary is doing ten years for some weed? Shit, that's a drag, man, wish I could do something. But you get your ass off the stage now, you fucking scumbag radical, before we call the police—we've had enough politics, man, and all we are saying is give peace a chance. Peace/love, baby, send Tim my regards, and maybe we can play a benefit in a couple months, after we get back off our tour. If our manager will let us, I mean.

But there's more to it than that, no matter how much or how many of you all want to throw all of that out of your minds and just have a good time, getting high and rockin' and rollin' and carryin' on. There's a lot more to it than that, the shit is coming down all over the world, and you are going to sound awfully fucking stupid trying to tell the heroic Vietnamese people that "the war is over if you want it" while they are being burned and bombed and blown out of their pitiful little huts and fields; you are going to sound awfully goddamn dumb telling that to Huey P. Newton, or to Bobby Seale, who they are trying to ease into the electric chair in Connecticut

44

right now; or to Fred Hampton's woman and his baby son; or to Lee Otis Johnson, who is doing thirty years for giving one joint to an undercover pig in Texas; you know what I mean? These people are not going to look on you as their friends when the people's inevitable response to the crushing repression of domestic imperialism starts; they are not going to be persuaded by a joint and a V-sign, you know? And they are going to have to look at you as just a bunch of silly freaks who are essentially no more far out than your fathers and Big Brothers, who they know are the real enemy. And they are going to blow your head off, groovy as it might seem to you (your head, that is).

And they will finally be right, because they know that the "owners," the people who control our lives and our destinies for the time being (but not for much longer!) are not going to be moved to give up their insane control and greed by a bunch of long-haired people sticking two fingers in the air and moaning "give peace a chance," no matter how groovy or how right these freaks are. These "owners" are too sick for that; it's going to take an organized effort by the people moving for their liberation to get the pigs off the stage of history; they are not going to be talked into capitulating—they are going to have to be pushed off that stage. Period. And either the people, the masses of the oppressed peoples of all the national minorities in the mother country—the youth, the black people, chicano people, native Americans, Puerto Rican-Americans—and their class allies the postindustrial working classes, either the people will be led by their natural vanguard, the musicians, poets, and artists, or they are going to go on for themselves and properly classify these creators as class traitors and fellow travelers of the pig, and deal with them as such. It's as simple as that, and as inevitable.

Because there is a war going on in this country right now, there is a war going on throughout the world, whether we like it or not, and there is no middle ground any more, for any of us. If you are not actively committed to the cause of freedom and self-determination for all peoples, which means that if you are not actively engaged in the struggle for freedom and self-determination by your own people, if your life itself is not dedicated to the people's struggle, if you do not live and breathe and struggle for freedom, not just for yourself, but for all people everywhere, then the people who *are* wholly involved in this struggle are forced to deal with you as part of the problem, no matter how distasteful this may seem to you. Because these people are not playing, *we* are not playing, this is as real as it gets, and if you can't relate to it, you will have to do like those other millionaires the Beatles, and "get back," and pray that this "sad song" will "get better," and hope that the people themselves will "let it be." And you might as well know it right now—they won't.

And the alternative is more than the Stones will have you believe, too—there's a lot more to our struggle than fighting in the streets or letting it bleed. There is the immense task of creative construction to be done, the task of building the new order in the standing ruins of the old, the task of building the life culture up from the ground and all the way out into the universe—and as Sun Ra has shown us, you don't need a rocket ship to get out there, you need discipline and commitment and determination, you need unity and dedication and power, you need an undying love for your people and for all people everywhere. You need what Sun Ra has made, has held up to us for almost twenty years in the incarnation of his mighty Arkestra and his incredible music, and you need this on the same every-day, day-after-day basis that Sun Ra has demonstrated it.

Because when we talk about self-determination in music, we have to start with Sun Ra and his Arkestra, and we have to examine that approach to the problem—that solution. Sun Ra's Arkestra is the most complete (and most completely beautiful) example of self-determination in music in all its modern history—the music is a *whole thing* with the musicians' lives, with Sun Ra's genius, with the revolutionary thrust for overall liberation and freedom on the planet and throughout the universe. Not very many people so far have even *heard* Sun Ra's astro-infinity music, or his myth-science music, or his solar music, or his intergalactic research music, or his astro-sonic music—not many people at all—but this music will last forever, and people are going to catch up with it once they get the chance to hear, which won't be long now, I will assure you. Because this music has to be heard, and felt, and followed . . . on out into space.

The two Sun Ra records listed in this review, *Strange Strings* and *Atlantis,* are two of the more than twenty albums produced and released on Sun Ra's self-determination label, Saturn Research (P.O. Box 7124, Chicago, Illinois 60607). When you send for them—because you won't be able to buy them at your local hip record store—Saturn Research is *not* "Entertainment from TransAmerica Corporation," or affiliated with any of the big defense/munitions companies like RCA, CBS, etc.—you should also send enough money for *The Magic City* album, one of the great masterpieces of all time. And you should also ask for some of the other Saturn favorites, including *When Angels Speak of Love,* or *When Sun Comes Out, Angels and Demons at Play, Sun Song,* et al. These recordings go back to 1955 or so, and continue up through tomorrow. The music is absolutely singular, and absolutely beautiful—the music of everybody's interstellar fantasies of space and the future. One of these records is worth more than thirteen moon shots; one Sun Ra is worth ten thousand astronauts, one million Richard Nixons.

After you start with Sun Ra and his Arkestra, if you are talking about self-determination music, the next people you have to deal with are the musicians and workers in the Association for the Advancement of Creative Musicians in Chicago. The AACM was written up in *Jazz & Pop,* a great article by Will Smith in the April 1970 issue, and you should know about it now—but I'm still afraid that you haven't got the records yet, and if you haven't, then you'd better start moving. The AACM is a practicing community of self-determination-minded musicians and other artists and workers, struggling for survival and teaching self-determination to young brothers and sisters in the black colony of Pig City, Chicago, teaching it by *practicing* it and by making it real in the music. The AACM maintains its own physical facility for teaching and practicing music, produces its own concerts and records, operates a functional music school in which the Association's musicians teach young people how to work instruments, how to compose and implement music, how to work together to make music and to make life freer and more liberating. The AACM is totally controlled by the musicians themselves, totally a product of their dedication and determination, and they place their work and their energies in the hands and at the service of the people of their community, which is what this is all about.

For the past four years or so, since 1966, the AACM has maintained a working relationship with the independent record company Delmark Records, owned and operated by blues enthusiast Bob Koester out of his Jazz Record Mart in Chicago (7 West Grand Street, Chicago 60610), and the AACM has made a great series of recordings with and for Delmark—including two albums by Joseph Jarman (*Song For* and *As If It Were the Seasons*), one by Roscoe Mitchell (*Sound*), one by saxophonist Anthony Braxton (*M-488: Three Compositions of New Jazz*), one by Richard Abrams (*Levels and Degrees of Light*), and now this milestone recording of Maurice McIntyre's music, *Humility in the Light of the Creator*, which is one of the strongest records of music to be released in some time.

Maurice's music is strong and powerful, as Maurice is, as the AACM is, as the people's aspirations are—LIFE FORCE, also the name of one of the songs, is the best single description of the music itself. And you have to get to *Melissa* and *Bismillah*, right now! The strong throat-chest voice of George Hines, John Stubblefield's soprano saxophone magic, Leo Smith's killer trumpet weight and light, sister Claudine Myers' heavy piano work, the all-powerful rhythm-drive team, and Maurice's steamroller tenor saxophone and clarinet—whew! "My music describes the coming of the Age of Aquarius," Maurice says, and he's not talking about *Hair* or the Fifth Dimension either. "That means we're living in a time of transition; the battles you see today, in the cities, for instance, are signs of the world adjusting to the new age." Just as this music is what Jarman called it, "Non-Cognitive Aspects of the city/where Roi J's prophesies become/the causes of children . . . /Long history upheaval . . . /Uppity the force of becoming/what art was made to return . . ."

These brothers—and sister Claudine—can play you RIGHT NOW, and they can work beyond that too, right straight into the future, and play it out for you just as they live it, just as they practice it, just as self-determination and the common vision are the force behind and within this music.

(Listening to Jarman's *Song For* as I write this, and I have to be sure that you *understand* how beautiful and how powerful this music is, in all its permutations—but you are going to have to *stand under* it, and take it into your bodies for your selves, and I hope you will do that.)

On this same level of self-determination, we have to deal next with the Liberation Music Orchestra and its natural brother or mother, the Jazz Composers Orchestra, which is another whole aspect of self-determination—different from the AACM, but shaped to the conditions of Death City, New York, which is different from Chicago and different from Los Angeles (which we will come to next) and different from Detroit (which you will be hearing about before you know it) and which has to be dealt with differently. The thing about self-determination is that it always has to deal uniquely with the selves involved, and each self (and each gathering of selves) is unique in itself, although the same principles apply—and the principles are that each self determines its own destiny, in line with the possibilities available to it under the objective conditions of its experience. Can you dig that? Because that's what's so beautiful about it, that *it is one with its source* and not something shaped by someone else to be forced on the source like a mold.

The Jazz Composers Orchestra has its own record label (JCOA) and produces its own concerts, pays all its members for rehearsals and performances, and operates its Jazz Composers Orchestra Association as a nonprofit corporation, all moneys going into a common fund to be used for the advancement of the JCOA as a whole. The Association is applying for federal-government grants and for economic assistance from the capitalist tax dodge, and maybe these institutions will make the mistake of giving up some money to this people's organization so it can institute further self-determination programs for the musicians involved in it; I hope so, but the JCOA will survive and grow either way, simply because it *has* to. Because these musicians are totally committed to the music, and to self-determination for themselves and for all people, and they will not be stopped.

Now, the Liberation Music Orchestra is not the Jazz Composers Orchestra; it is an offshot of the JCO which was put together to make this record for Impulse Records; the Jazz Composers Orchestra, as I understand it, will record only under its own auspices, on its own label, and under its own conditions, which is right on. And to understand that, we should go back to the beginnings of the organization, and its forerunner, which was known as the Jazz Composers Guild, a cooperative organization of New York musicians which was formed along strict self-determination lines in 1964, by people like Sun Ra, Mike Mantler, Carla Bley, Archie Shepp, Cecil Taylor, Bill Dixon, Roswell Rudd, John Tchicai, Burton Greene, and Paul Bley. The idea was that the revolutionary musicians of New York City, the whole panoply of the jazz avant-garde, had gathered together to create a situation for themselves and their possible listeners and participants, a working and performing and even recording situation based on complete economic self-determination for the artist. They rented their own JCG loft and were trying to put together their own recording company; they produced their own concerts—including two historic rounds called the October Revolution and the Four Days in December, both in 1964; and they arrived at all decisions collectively within the organization. They had an agreement within the Guild that no one artist or group would record or even take commercial gigs unless the contracts and the circumstances of the employment met with the approval of the whole Guild, in other words, the whole thing was a collective cooperative operation, and it was almost too good to be true.

In fact, as events proved, it *was* too good to be true finally, and the original Guild broke up in 1965 after a great deal of hassling among the members. It seemed to me at the time that New York itself was largely responsible for the collapse of the Guild, the pressures of that incredibly intense competitive-consumer-capitalist scene, and the people involved just weren't ready for such a momentous move. Their *theory* was really together, but they couldn't sustain it in *practice*, and the immediate possibility of the Guild wasn't really realized. But the Guild's brief history, and especially the principles upon which it was founded, had a tremendous effect on people all over the country, and I'm sure I'm not wrong in saying that its influence is still being heavily felt, and manifested, in other self-determination jazz groups such as the AACM in Chicago, the UMAA group in Los Angeles, the (now defunct) Artist's Workshop (which is reemerging, so I'm told, under a different name, as a whole new all-musician collective operation with a much broader base than the Workshop had, which is really good news for everyone concerned), and other people who were directly inspired by the Guild. Certainly its effect is still strong in New York in the existence of the JCOA, which is a direct outgrowth of the original Guild, although its aims and goals aren't quite so ambitious, and it is using different and more effective means now for achieving its goals.

Anyway, I didn't want to talk about the Liberation Music Orchestra without dealing with its parent association, because the LMO's record is more than just another great album release—it is a partial record of the energies and resources which make up the larger body, the JCOA, and it will have to be recognized as such. As for the music, on the Liberation Music record, it is a different thing from the music of the JCO, a thing of its own definition, programmatic in this instance, the theme being, as Charlie Haden puts it, "Creating a better world—a world without war and killing, without racism, without poverty and exploitation; a world where men of all governments realize the vital importance of life and strive to protect rather than to destroy it. We hope to see a new society of enlightenment and wisdom where creative thought becomes the most dominant force in all people's lives." Right on, Charlie Haden, right on, brother!

The songs, which have been arranged by Carla Bley (a dynamite arranger, I must add), are drawn from international sources—the Spanish Civil War, the Cuban Revolution (*Song for Che*), the "civil-rights" struggle in Amerika, the youth rebellion (*Circus '68 '69*), and the internationalist imperialist slaughter (*War Orphans*, composed by Ornette Coleman)— and brought into the single context of *Liberation*, which is as it always should be. All of the musicians are outstanding; the multimedia effects (where voices and chants are woven into the instrumental music of *Che* and in and out of the *Song of the United Front*) are beautifully done; Haden's life-force bass work is outstanding throughout (especially on *Che*), Rudd's trombone, Barbieri, Carla's piano work, Don Cherry ("bright," as always), Sam Brown's guitar touches (which in their use here are highly reminiscent of Mingus' *Black Saint and the Sinner Lady*, another great masterpiece of modern music)—the whole thing is tremendous, beautifully done, and beautifully put together.

(Now that I said "Mingus" back there, I have to say something about that man too, because in a lot of ways he has been in the vanguard of the self-determination movement in jazz for years—as far back as the Debut recordings of the early fifties, and the Jazz Workshop concept he developed through the fifties and sixties, and the creation of his own Charles Mingus record label later in the sixties—all of this, plus the incredible force of his music through all of these years. Mingus is too often ignored and overlooked, and we can't do that anymore—the brother is too powerful to pass over like that, too powerful and too inspirational for too many people. In fact, you will hear and feel a lot of the spirit of

Mingus' orchestra work here in this record, *Liberation Music Orchestra*, which is only proper, after all).*

*The need for economic self-determination and the destruction of corporate capitalism is very clearly demonstrated by circumstances which surrounded the making of *Liberation Music Orchestra*. Robert Levin reported on those circumstances in the July 1970 issue of *Jazz & Pop*.

"Ornette Coleman's bassist Charlie Haden conceived the idea for *Liberation Music Orchestra* . . . some five years ago, after hearing a record of Spanish Civil War songs and seeing the film *To Die in Madrid*. He was moved to pay tribute to the resistance of the Spanish Republic against the fascist forces of Franco, Mussolini, and Hitler, and to the 3,000 men from the United States who volunteered to fight for the Republic. (Half of those Americans were killed in the ill-fated struggle; the rest returned to this country—which had maintained a probably decisive neutrality—only to be vilified as communists.) More recently Haden decided that he wanted to include a statement about incipient American fascism.

"Haden's concept was to take Spanish songs that were popular during the war (in several instances actual tapes from the 1930's), contemporary revolutionary ballads, and (on a track called *Circus* which endeavors to communicate the evil, chaos, and horror of the 1968 Democratic Convention) songs like *You're a Grand Old Flag*, *Happy Days Are Here Again*, and *We Shall Overcome*, and to mix—variously interpolate, superimpose, juxtapose—these with original material and a "free" jazz expression.

"To say that Haden ran into difficulties getting his project accomplished would be to drastically understate the adversities he encountered. Determining what he wanted to do and how he wanted to do it, and gathering the right new-tradition-oriented musicians was not half the battle; it meant only that a battle would begin.

"It took Haden two years to persuade a record company to sponsor his album (the integrity of which from the nature of the music to the title to the inclusion of blatantly left-wing liner notes, he refused to compromise). When he finally did record (in the spring of 1969 at Judson Hall before a small, invited audience), the budget was so tight that he was forced to tape complex music in just three brief sessions and with next to no rehearsal time. The problem of limited time was compounded when the wrong equipment was used at the first session, making it necessary to re-record everything that had been played that day. Moreover, Haden reports that throughout the sessions he and his musicians experienced a distinct hostility toward the project from the Impulse (ABC Paramount) people. The tensions, he says, were hardly conducive to creativity. At one point during the taping Carla Bley became seriously ill; on another day Don Cherry left in tears.

"Recording the album did not mean Haden was home free. Not yet. Impulse executives were reluctant to antagonize their stockholders by putting such an album on the market under their trademark. To get the set released, Haden was compelled to make a special, personally

financed trip to the West Coast where the Impulse offices are located and
to demand that it be issued.

"Another problem was promotion. Haden, despite Impulse's considerable publicity machinery, was forced to send out review copies and
cajole air time from disc jockeys himself.

"Although the album enjoyed pretty decent sales almost immediately,
was very well received by critics, and won a couple of international awards,
it was not advertised until months after its release, and only after heavy
pressure was applied by Haden and the jazz and rock press.

"Haden, although he says he is satisfied that *Liberation Music
Orchestra* is an artistically successful record, speaks with rancor about
the circumstances under which it was made. Bob Thiele, who produced
the set shortly before leaving Impulse and starting Flying Dutchman, and
who has been the object of much of Haden's bitterness, describes the
circumstances from his perspective:

" 'When Charlie came to me with the idea I thought it was great
and I said we'd try to do it. I went to see the brass at ABC and discussed
it with them. They were initially reluctant for three reasons: first of all,
they said, no one had heard of Charlie Haden; secondly, they thought he
was asking for too much money. Finally, they said, they were concerned
about the subject matter. I told Charlie this, and to say he was persistent
is putting it mildly. He persuaded me to keep pushing, and eventually I
was able to get approval. The money was less than Charlie felt he needed
to do the album right, but we agreed that we could make do with it.

" 'Charlie hasn't spoken more than two words to me since the recording sessions, and without me the record would never have been made
because of the politics involved. We were on a very strict budget, and
there is never enough time to get what you want, but by the time we did
the sessions, after fighting to be able to do the album, I was very committed to it myself. At the sessions a lot of time was going by while
everyone sat around having sandwiches and talking. I wanted Charlie to
have a relaxed atmosphere, but the age-old problem of a tight budget
and not enough time made it necessary for me to say, "C'mon, let's get
to it." Everyone resented that. Bob Northern said to me. "You don't
understand, this music"— he pointed to his heart—"comes from here,
and it will happen when it happens." I was fighting for Charlie, but I
was also representing ABC, and I had to get things moving.

" 'Charlie . . . can't accept the fact that money and time problems
exist for everyone—they even existed on Coltrane dates. . . . Later I
arranged for Charlie to do the mixing, which was against ABC policy.
Then there was a battle about the word "liberation" being used in the
title. ABC said it sounded left-wing. I said the word was beautiful and
didn't have anything to do with left-wing or right-wing. They said that
today the word had a communist connotation. I fought and kept the word
for Haden. When I left the company, he had no one to fight for him,
and he had to take care of things himself. The average record buyer has
no idea of the shit that goes down with record companies. I don't know
how to correct the situation, but sometimes the blame gets put on the
wrong person.' "

After the Liberation record, we have to move to the Los Angeles area to deal with some of its revolutionary artifacts—Horace Tapscott's album *The Giant Is Awakened; Seize the Time*, by Elaine Brown, with an orchestra arranged and conducted by H. Tapscott; and Stanley Crouch's record of poetry, prose, and cultural history called *Ain't No Ambulances fo No Nigguhs Tonight*. All three of these records go together in more ways than one, because they are an expression of the spirit of the black colony in Watts-Southern California, an expression of the people's need for self-determination, and they are each and all three very important records to have available.

I want to talk about Horace Tapscott's record first, if just briefly, because *The Giant Is Awakened* is another one of the purest and finest albums of music that has been released in a long time. You have to hear this record. I had been reading and hearing about the Los Angeles self-determination movement for some time, but I didn't imagine really that it would be so together until I heard this album by Horace Tapscott and Black Arthur Blythe and their brothers, which is a fully realized, wholly exciting, masterfully conceived and executed recording of contemporary music. Nothing I can say about it will do it justice—you have to listen to it for that, you have to listen to Black Arthur *deal* with that alto saxophone, and to Tapscott's driving piano work, the total drum drive of Everett Brown, Jr., the churning bass work, the compositions, which are something again in themselves, the range and scope of this music—you have to hear all this, take it into yourselves, and feel it there, to get full justice from it. And this music, this awakened giant, will help wake up that giant inside you all too, help wake you and shake you and bring you to the commitment these men have to their people, to all people, struggling to be free.

Horace and Black Arthur and Stanley Crouch and Carter-Bradford & Co. and other musicians and poets and creators are involved in a cultural self-determination movement in the Los Angeles area which I believe is called the Underground Musicians and Artists Association, which is right on. Elaine

Brown, on the other hand—or farther out on the same hand is probably the best way to put it within the scope of that metaphor—is deputy minister of information for the Black Panther party, Southern California chapter, which makes her part of a movement which is committed to the self-determination of all peoples in every aspect of their lives. And her record here, *Seize the Time*, is issued as part of her work in the Information Ministry, and as such goes with Eldridge Cleaver's books and other writings, and the *Black Panther* newspaper, and the community information centers organized and manned by the Black Panther party, and the Black Community News Service as a whole, because of all these things and artifacts—and I might mention a great record by Eldridge, too, which is called *Dig* and is available through the Ministry of Information, Black Panther party, Box 2967, Custom House, San Francisco, California 94126, as is the newspaper, and Elaine's album too—are part of the same work, and that is the work of informing the people of the real conditions which obtain in this country and what can be done about them, what solutions are available, and how these solutions can be implemented.

As I said, Elaine Brown's record is to be taken in the context of the Black Panther party as well. The Black Panther party is the vanguard organization in North America in the people's struggle for self-determination. When we talk about self-determination in America we have to talk about the Black Panther party, we have to talk about Huey P. Newton, we have to talk about Bobby Seale, Chairman Bobby, we have to talk about Eldridge Cleaver and the Panther 21 and the murdered brothers, Fred Hampton, Bobby Hutton, John Huggins, Bunchy Carter, we have to talk about the New Haven 8 on trial right now, heroic sister Erika Huggins and her New Haven chapter, we have to talk about the Free Breakfast for Children program and the Free Medical Care Center program, the National Committee to Combat Fascism, and revolutionary self-determination for all people on all levels. And this record is just one tiny manifestation of the party's program for self-determination.

The music itself isn't as strong as the other musics discussed in this review, although it was arranged for an orchestra by Horace Tapscott and conducted by brother Tapscott—but maybe that's the trouble, because the songs themselves, all of them composed by sister Elaine, are lean, hard songs which deserve better (stronger) musical settings than have been provided for them here on this record. But you would be making a mistake to pass up this record, because you have to hear the songs on here to get a sense of the direction in which our music, and especially our songwriters, must go in the immediate future. *Seize the Time*, especially, is something all of us have to relate to, and the only way to get it now is to pick up on this record and plug in to it.

I do have to mention the one reservation I have, and that is that the arrangements and orchestration here are not entirely what they should be, but it's still beautiful to see Horace Tapscott aligned with sister Elaine and the party on this project, just as it was beautiful to see the heaviest musicians in New York City all playing at a benefit for the Panther 21 a few weeks ago, a benefit which was organized and produced by Calvin Massey, just as it was beautiful that Archie Shepp & Co. played in New Haven with and for the Panthers. Because our artists and musicians, no matter how beautiful their own self-determination programs are, must align themselves with the brothers and sisters who are working in the streets and in the neighborhoods and the colonies for the liberation of the people, or else their music will just be so much empty noise finally. It's just as Chairman Mao has said, "In the world today all cultures, all literature and art belong to definite classes and are geared to definite political lines. There is in fact no such thing as art for art's sake, art that stands above classes, art that is detached from or independent of politics." Art is either in the service of the people, or it is contributing to the people's oppression. Again, I know people don't wanna hear this, but

I have to say it, and people are going to have to start relating to it.

Stanley Crouch will tell you the same thing when you listen to his album—it starts out with a brilliant rap on cultural repression in which he tries to explain some very basic things about black culture to an audience of what would seem to be mostly black students of middle-class origin, and he tries to explain to them (and to you) just why it is that they (and you) are familiar with certain popular or public performing artists and not at all familiar with others—*e.g.*, Dave Brubeck as against Tricky Sam Nanton, Janis Joplin as against Howlin' Wolf, Gerry Mulligan as against Black Arthur Blythe. And he's absolutely right, which must be taken into account at all times, because, again, there is no separation between art and the rest of reality, everything has to do with it, as Trane said, and there are certainly *reasons* why we know this one thing and not another thing, or why we are *given* to know one thing, where we are not given to know another. Stanley is a very persuasive speaker, and his prose (a *moving*, as, it moves, and it will move you, passage from a novel he has written) and poetry (which I won't even quote here, because I want you to get this record and hear it for yourself) are even more together than his rap, which is right on. This is an important recording to have been released, and I hope there will be more of them.

There is one reservation I had with this record too, although in terms of the whole album it's really a minor one, but I have to put it in here because it has to do with everything else I've been talking about in here—and that is the inaccurate and I would have to say unnecessary racial chauvinism Stanley Crouch brings out in the course of his rap, putting down a sister like Janis Joplin for the wrong reasons, and failing to distinguish between the revolutionary culture of the mostly white youth colony—which is sympathetic to and which in fact has been inspired by the black colony and its culture—and the reactionary, decadent culture of the plastic honko death society of Pat Boone and Dinah Shore and Spiro T. Agnew and their ilk. But still his rap is beautiful and necessary, and these things can and must be excused, because he was making some very important points with his brothers and sisters who have been brought up in that death culture and robbed of all knowledge and experience of the most vital aspects of their own (black colonial) culture in Amerika. And it is more important at this stage for poet-warriors like Stanley Crouch to help their (black) people restore the sense of culture heritage which has been denied them so long than it is to put Janis Joplin in her place for the right reasons, which is, that she has allowed herself to be victimized and brutalized by the death merchants and star-makers, ripped off from *her* people (of the youth colony) and her cultural experience and used instead *against* the culture she helped to create, used by the rock-and-roll imperialists to keep the rising youth natives in their place, which is at the ticket office and the cash register of the record stores and box offices. But she will still come back to her people as soon as the pigs lose interest in her and she comes to see that they have just been exploiting her, because she's a righteous sister and she sure can *sing*, and we need her too bad to let her stay away like that—and she needs us too!*

I wish I had more time and space here to talk about that problem, because all of us in the youth colony have to start relating to what's happening to our music and our culture as the rock-pop imperialists move to monopolize our energies and resources and use them against us—I would say our money too, but that's the least important part of it. They drain us of our righteous strengths, and they take our artists and performers and turn them against our struggle for freedom and self-determination, and they train them to tell our people that our lives have nothing to do with—ugh!—"politics." They do that, and we have to stop it. That's why I write shit like this; I mean, I would rather just talk about the music, you dig, but then I'd rather just be home with my people than in the penitentiary doing 9½–10 years for getting high, and I would rather that

*Janis Joplin died October 4, 1970, two months after this piece was printed.

John Sinclair

they would just give peace a chance too, but we have to deal with this shit the way it comes down on us, and we have to see that it's all connected, that separation *is* doom for us, that we are not going to be free *individually* until *all* the people are free *collectively*. Dig it.

All of this has to do with Stanley Crouch's great record, which you will have to *hear*, because I'm not going to quote you things from it—it's made to be *heard*, not read. And you have to hear it, but please hear it in this context, in the context that it is another blow for self-determination, another weapon in the cultural revolution, another move for the people's liberation. And then you will hear it properly.

There is one more spoken record that I have to get in here too, before I finish with the last two music records: that record is *A Night at Santa Rita*, and it has to do with self-determination on two important levels: one, that it is a record of what happened to over four hundred brothers and sisters in Berkeley just over a year ago as a result of their struggles with the pig power structure over the issue of People's Park, as a result of the Battle of People's Park, which was a classic self-determination move by the youth colony out there, and which was met with the most brutal resistance by the established order in California just because the brothers and sisters were striking so close to home by moving to liberate an unused piece of government land and use it for the people, to create a People's Park on this land and turn the Park over to all the people to use as they see fit. You can get the story on the record and on the record jacket, and you should know about it already anyway, because we have to be aware of our own history, and if you don't know what's happening in this country right now, if you can't relate to the rise of fascism in the United States of Amerika, then you will really have to get this record and hear the story of just one incident in the current fascist campaign for yourself.

And the other level is that this album of *A Night at Santa Rita*, which is a very important record and which represents a very important new development in the record industry—getting hard-core information on American fascism to the mass record-buying public—this record was conceived and produced and marketed in another type of self-determination approach, by Bob Thiele and his Flying Dutchman operation, an approach which has been the most prevalent in the music business so far as self-determination efforts are concerned—the independent company—but which has not until now been fully utilized in the people's cause. I mean there have been, and are, independently owned record companies and (many more) production companies—some of them strictly profit-oriented—but until Thiele formed Flying Dutchman and undertook the program he is involved in now, which is typified by the *Santa Rita* album, there hasn't been an independent company which is almost wholly given to independent music and spoken word releases, which is given not only to self-determination for the producer-marketer and perhaps for the artist but also to self-determination for the people as a whole, and which commitment is manifested by a program which works to inform and educate the people and consistently to raise their consciousness.

Thiele has made the turn, and it's a big step in the right direction. I am not going to try to make a case for Bob Thiele as a people's hero, and I'm sure he wouldn't want to make that kind of postulation either, but I am going to insist that—whatever you think his motives might be—the *effect* of Thiele's move is a revolutionary one, and opens the way to a greater availability of mass-media technology for more revolutionary musicians and other artists who have not had access to the people's ears before. I mean that Thiele has taken chances that established record companies have refused to take, for fear of diminished profits or repressive measures by commercial and/or government interests, and which other independent companies have not really been interested in, or have not been able to bring to the attention of a mass public once such steps *are* taken (and I'm thinking particularly of ESP-Disk, which has not been afraid to publish what the established companies have always considered as controversial language or music— Douglas Records is another instance—but companies such as these have not been able to publicize and advertise their product extensively, and in the popular entertainment market, advertising and publicity are the *crucial* factors in selling records, much more important than the music itself).

Thiele's program—which includes the *Santa Rita* album and an equally important record on the My Lai massacres, as well as the Horace Tapscott, Gato Barbieri, Leon Thomas, Bobby Bradford-John Carter records—is a dangerous one, and it is a true self-determination program which can only aid the people's liberation struggle. It's not the highest form of self-determination in the arts—I have to insist that Sun Ra's operation is the highest form, and that musicians' cooperatives like the AACM, JCOA, and UMAA groups are the next highest form, and that revolutionary rock-and-roll-band operations like the Up and a very few others are in the most advanced stage of development—but it is a *significant* form which adds considerably to the scope of the self-determination movement.

O.K. The last two records are *Black Woman*, by Sonny Sharrock & Co., and *Daddy Bug*, by Roy Ayers, with strings and woodwinds, and I include them in this survey because they represent still another secondary form of artistic self-determination, the independent production operation which has access to the mass market through distribution agreements with stone capitalistic companies. Both of these records were produced by Herbie Mann under his new independent-production operation, and they represent his commitment to take the role of the bandleader and employer another step further by looking out for the interests of his sidemen and developing their individual talents and thrusts as far as possible. Sharrock and Ayers both work regularly in Mann's extremely popular band, and he has made a commitment to them which is very much to the benefit of his employees. Already (*i.e.*, since these two records were made, and released on Atlantic's label) Mann has created his own company, Embryo, which is released through Atlantic, and has produced recordings by other members of his band and some other people, including Ron Carter and a rock band Mann manages, called Brute Force.

This is not a revolutionary form of self-determination, since the music is not revolutionary music except by chance, *i.e.*, there may or may not be revolutionary musicians working for Mann; if there are, then they will get to record their music under Mann's self-determination program and thus gain some attention for themselves, so they can move out from where they are into a more liberated position, like forming their own working band and eventually, perhaps, their own record companies, etc. Mann's music itself is high-quality commercial music, and his operation is a high-quality commercial operation, but it's a step in the right direction and it opens up new possibilities for more people to get to their highest levels of creativity and production.

Sonny Sharrock is an extremely *progressive* musician, in his associations (Pharaoh Sanders in particular) and in his actual guitar playing and group composing, but he isn't yet a fully *revolutionary* artist, even though his thrusts are certainly in that direction. This first record of his, *Black Woman*, represents Sonny Sharrock accurately, I think, and shows that he hasn't got it all together yet but that he's going to do that. He has put together a dynamite band for this record—Dave Burrell, Norris Jones, and Milford Graves, plus his wife, Linda, on voice and Teddy Daniels on trumpet—and he has advanced some killer musical directions, particularly in his uses of Linda's voice (the song *Black Woman*, especially) and of his cultural heritage (*Blind Willy*), which is a dangerous blues translation, and his *Portrait of Linda in Three Colors, All Black*). Linda's vocal music is in the same *field* as that opened up (on record anyway) by Patty Waters (and if you don't know her record *Black Is the Color*, then you had better find it soon), but I don't want even to suggest that Linda Sharrock could be a follower of Patty Waters—she's entirely her own self, and she sings that self on the record. It's just that there are so few sisters, and just as few brothers (and I will direct you back to George Hines, on Maurice McIntyre's record, and brother Leon Thomas, and not many others) who are into the open field of vocal music as Pharaoh Sanders and

Archie Shepp and Albert Ayler, say, are into the open field of horn music, or as Cecil Taylor and Sun Ra and Carla Bley, for examples, are into the open field of piano music. Which is not to say that anyone sounds *like* someone else in the field, but that the field is *open* and admits of infinite variety. And that this vocal music—as presented by Linda Sharrock on this record—is to the popular vocal music we are accustomed to as Archie Shepp, say, is to Lou Donaldson, or Albert Ayler to Sonny Stitt. Which is not to make any cheap disparagements, but simply to suggest the essential *difference* involved. I shouldn't verbalize all this to such an extent, because once you *listen* to Linda Sharrock (or Patty Waters, or George Hines, or Leon Thomas), you will understand just what I mean. They move directly with their pulse and feeling, and with the openness of the music, and consequently open up a bigger space for the registration of direct human feeling, which can reach *us* that much more directly. Yes. They open up new possibilities, and what is more to the point, they make use of them so beautifully.

Because there are always two things involved: *opening up* the possibilities inherent in the music (or in one's life), in the instruments, and in the body itself; and *realizing* those possibilities as fully as they suggest they can be realized. And what I was starting to say about Sonny Sharrock's record is that it isn't fully realized, that the possibilities it suggests are not fully developed, that it is decidely a *first* record of his music, an opening shot and very exciting for that, but not a *complete* record, which is only to say that it sounds like we *will* get a complete record maybe the next time, you know? Sonny has really opened up a lot of space for guitar players—and all rock-and-roll guitarists should be checking out the possibilities that Sonny has been working out—to work in; his approach to the instrument in this open-field high-energy music is entirely strong and unique and moving; his musical composition and direction are exciting; his partnership on records with his wife, Linda, is bound to take us all somewhere else together when they get it all together; and we have to thank Herbie Mann and his farsighted "vanguard-capitalism" concept for giving Sonny and his band this opening.

Now, Roy Ayers' music is wholly different from the rest of the music and words I have been talking about in this piece; it's a more strictly commercial music, using established, popular forms and concepts and embellishing them to make some money and some people feel nicer than they do now—not adventurous or revolutionary music at all, but good *refined* music meant for the big money market and the pop-jazz audience. "High-energy Muzak" is what I would have to characterize it as, and hope you can relate to that. I only include it here because it—Ayers' record—is part of Herbie Mann's program, and it was sent to me to review. I like it and all, but it doesn't have anything more than that to do with the music or the lives or the struggles I have given this writing to.

I have to get out of this piece without being able to talk about the self-determination movement as completely as it should be discussed, but I've taken up too much space already and will have to let this go as what it is, a sketchy primer on self-determination, and music as it is, present (represented) in some recent record releases. There is much more to be said on this whole question of self-determination in music, but it will have to wait for another time.

I just want to summarize here some of the things that I've tried to deal with in this essay, and point out how the approaches and solutions to the problem of self-determination developed by the musicians and producers described here can be used by other musicians and other people in the industry who want to move themselves for self-determination, who want to serve the people's cause through their work in the mass entertainment industry. First, you can form your own revolutionary musical units, or bands, and establish the means by which you can control your production—cooperative booking agencies; cooperative production alliances, both for recordings and for life gigs; cooperative living arrangements where all the members of a band, including management, publicity, design workers, and anyone else who works with the band, all *live* together and work at the highest level of collectivism to produce revolutionary music with a revolutionary effect. This is self-determination on the primary, or highest, level. And this form of self-determination, which initially affects only the band and workers themselves, can be extended to all the people by using this situation to produce only revolutionary music (high-energy CHANGE music) in revolutionary situations, *e.g.*, by performing for benefits and other worthwhile causes as much as possible; by setting up your own concert/dances on a revolutionary (total-involvement) model rather than the typical Hollywood-capitalist model which crams as many people as possible into an auditorium, charges them high prices to get in, and presents the "acts" as if it were a movie or a Hollywood entertainment event; and by using the opportunity to reach the masses of people that the entertainment industry presents, by using this opportunity to educate and organize the people and to give them information which they need to know, rather than just going through an act for forty-five minutes or an hour, collecting the bread, and going home. On this level of self-determination, the music itself is revolutionary, the music is a direct extension of the musicians' revolutionary lives, and everything the band does presents a revolutionary alternative to the people who encounter the band and/or its music. And the beautiful thing about this total revolutionary approach is that it is available to anyone who wants to do more than just make some records, thrill the fans, and get the money. Any band can do it, once they decide that they want to serve the people rather than the people's oppressors; and the more bands that do it, the better the music will be and the more people will be led toward the road of liberation and self-determination.

Another approach to the problem is through the formation of economic cooperatives for musicians—organizations in which musicians of various persuasions and directions gather together to determine their own destinies through controlling their performance situations, their record contracts, and even their recordings. All kinds of bands, whether they are revolutionary in purpose and/or effect or not, can involve themselves in this type of "united-front" activity and help each other gain control over the productive aspects of their work. The Jazz Composers Orchestra, the AACM, the UMAA, the new cooperative jazz musicians' group in Detroit, are all examples of this type of self-determination program. And again, this type of activity can be entered into by any band or group once it determines that it's more interested in self-determination than in BIG FAME AND MONEY. And I should make it clear that neither one of the approaches precludes the possibility of getting the big buck in the biz; but it usually happens that once you get into the consciousness which produces these approaches, you usually don't care too much about "making it" in the Hollywood sense. You still want to reach as many people as possible, but you also want to make sure that you still have something important and strong and beautiful to say to them—because you realize that the consumer culture eats up beauty and destroys it along the way, that it takes people who have something to say and shuts them up without them even being aware of it. And you want to be aware of *everything* by the time you achieve this level of consciousness!

A third approach is the independent-production step, by means of which one musician or producer sets up an organization to control the production of music by himself, his group, and/or his friends or people he admires and wants to introduce to the public. Bob Thiele's Flying Dutchman operation is an example of the producer-owned independent-production company; Herbie Mann's Embryo company is an example of the musician-owned independent-production operation. Both of these approaches are considerably more useful to the people than the standard monopolist/corporate deal by means of which most records and other musical artifacts are produced and marketed. You have to have some capital—a solid reputation and "track record" in the biz, a big entertainment name which will help sell records, etc.—in order to set up this type of operation, but now more and more performers are getting access to both capital and fame, and the need is that they start using it to help their brothers and sisters by supporting self-determination programs of all types.

Again, I have to make the distinction between revolutionary and nonrevolutionary developments in this particular area, because the independent-production approach is not intrinsically a revolutionary form, although it can easily be used in a revolutionary manner by a revolutionary artist or producer. The measure is that the revolutionary, or potentially revolutionary, independent-production operation produces revolutionary music and revolutionary artists, while the nonrevolutionary independent-production company produces nonrevolutionary (bourgeois) forms of music and art. Flying Dutchman is a good example of the first, or potentially revolutionary, type; Mann's Embryo is an example of a nonrevolutionary operation with revolutionary possibilities now only hinted at (Sharrock's record); and the Beatles' Apple Corps Ltd. is an example of a distinctly non- or antirevolutionary company, producing such superb examples of bourgeois art as *Postcard* by Mary Hopkins, *Magic Christian Music* by Badfinger, *Space* by the MJQ, and the Beatles' releases such as *Let It Be* and *Abbey Road*.

These are some of the alternatives available to young musicians who want to commit themselves as artists to the cause of the people but don't know how to do it. These are some alternatives that nonmusicians but heavy users of music and the new culture can relate to and support. These are some of the alternatives all of us should be aware of so we can start moving to free ourselves and our culture(s) from the grasp of the pig. We have to come up with new ways to control our own production, to determine our own destinies, and we have to support new and human alternatives when they arise, and learn from them. Because we have self-determination, and we have to have it for everybody, on every level. All Power to the People! We are not free until all the people are free! Long Live the People's Revolutionary Culture!

ROBERT LEVIN

1971

Going Outside

(as told to Robert Levin by Sunny Murray*)

For a while there were a lot of people trying to kill me.

See, it began a short time after I met Cecil Taylor—who is like the father of the New Black Music. I met him at a little place in the West Village called the Café Roué. It was in the winter of 1959. I came in one night with a cat named Wade, who had just bought a bass yesterday. All the bebop dudes that I used to play with were there. Cecil came in a few minutes later and sat in a corner with his collar up over his head. All the dudes immediately started packing up, and when I asked them why, they said, "You don't know Cecil Taylor; the way he plays, can't nobody get together with him."

Well, you know, I've always admired a cat that stood out in a crowd, because it meant he was very . . . very *useful*. He was a necessity. He wasn't one to shun, he was one to dig. And I thought, if you pack up when a man comes in to play, then he must be *something*. Let some more come in that make you pack up, and I'll be around some really good musicians.

*Sunny Murray has been the major drum force in the New Black Music.

It was like when I was hanging out on the corner with the guys in Philadelphia. If a cat would come up who the other cats didn't like, I'd want to know why. And if they gave me some sick-assed reason, I'd say to the cat who'd come up, "Let's you and me split," and I'd leave *them* there. So I said, "Listen, man, I'm going to play with him." And they said, "Go ahead, we will listen."

So I went over to Cecil and introduced myself and said, "I would like to play with you." And he said, "Do you know how I play?" And I said, "No." He said, "Are you *sure* you want to play with me?" I said, "Yeah." He took off his coat, and everybody got all tense, and he went to the piano and started playing.

Well, you know, in '59 it *was* a little different. I said to myself, damn, he sure *is* into something else, and I struggled along. But I played a whole three tunes. Wade played too, even though he couldn't really play. Cecil said, "That's all right, let him do it if he wants." Cecil laughed. He had fun. A couple times I didn't know what to do, and I just stopped, and Cecil turned around and said, "No, keep going, don't stop." I wasn't just playing conventional, like *tanka-ting*—I could have, but I decided not to play that way with him. I was playing on one. Like Elvin Jones was playing on one in Detroit, but I didn't know about him yet. I just thought it was hip to play on one. Bass players would always say, "Oh, mother-fucker, you keep turning the beat around." So a lot of cats didn't like me, though some cats did.

I went back to play with the beboppers after that night, and they all started laughing and kept saying, "Hey, Sunny played with Cecil, Sunny played with Cecil," and making a big joke out of it. And I was thinking, who *is* Cecil? Who the devil *is* this cat I played with? And I looked for Cecil, man, for days, every day. I thought, I ain't heard nobody play like that, and I'm gonna make sure that I can play with him again, 'cause I knew he had enjoyed my playing and it wasn't like I was bugging his nerves.

Finally I found Cecil at the old Cedar Bar. He helped me get a loft on Dey Street in a building where he was living. After I moved in, I knocked on his door. There was no answer, but as it happened, we both had the same set of keys. I opened the door and brought my drums in after me. Cecil was lying in bed looking at me. It was a depressing period for him, nobody wanted to play with him. I said, "You don't mind?" And he said, "Uh-um." And I set 'em up. But I was too nervous to start playing with the cat in bed. It took me about three weeks to decide, well, I'm gonna play anyway. I've got to practice, and my drums is over there now, and he said, "O.K." So I played, but he wouldn't get out of bed, and his windows was open, and snow was on the windowsill up about twelve inches, and I'd be trying to talk to him and shivering, and finally I said, "I can't talk to you like this. Can I please close your windows?" And he said, "O.K." I'd been practicing there with a big coat on, and I was getting tired of it.

Finally, one day, Cecil did get up to play with me. He got up to play on his old, beat-up upright piano and said, "I want you to play something like you never played before." I said, "What do you mean, like a drum solo?" And I started to play a drum solo, and Cecil said, "No. Stop. Just . . . let yourself play." Just let myself play. I thought that was kind of weird at first. But you understand what he meant by "just let yourself play." He meant like not to be hung up on artificial rules and roles and disciplines and orders that have been set up and which limit what you can express—or to be daring or hip while *still staying within the confines of those rules,* you know, like playing on one. He meant like to go outside of those rules and roles, you know what I'm saying, like to go outside of "time" and to play *naturally*—out of the *natural rules and rhythms of my body.* Also to really listen to him and to play *with* him, not just behind him as an accompanist. Dig all the energy that is liberated with this kind of playing, and the things that can happen when two or three or four or a dozen cats are playing together like that. The spiritual things that can happen, that you can get to. Like if Charlie Parker had *really* let himself go twenty-five years ago, we would be past all the shit by now and really out there. This is a whole new freedom and a whole new *system* of music. And dig the revolutionary . . . *enormity* of it.

Of course, I have to admit that I didn't understand all of this right away. I was the first drummer to play the New Black Music, the New Jazz, and for a long time I wasn't really sure about what I was doing. It seemed like what I was playing was *un*natural, not natural. I was very disturbed. I used to listen to tapes of myself and wonder if I was going crazy.

It was really about three years until I really understood that Cecil was leading me into a new system. Those were a very difficult three years for me, particularly because of all the attempts on my life that happened during this period.

Like I went over to the Village Vanguard one night—I was living over on West Eleventh Street then—and I got into a discussion with some dude about the music, and he said that this music was crazy and would never survive. I laughed him off and went outside. But when I got to the corner, there was a Thunderbird parked there with the lights on real bright. Something said to me, don't walk in front of that car, that's the dude you were arguing with. I thought I was being paranoid, so I walked in front of the car. And Jim, if it wasn't a fucking movie scene! I had to dive, and landed right on my fucking ass. The car took off. I got up and just stood there, and I thought, why the fuck do they want to run me over? I started to walk toward my house, and I saw the car again turning a corner coming toward me. I ran into the house, and I went into a vacant apartment. There wasn't nothing there but a mattress— wasn't even no lock on the door. I looked out the window, and there's two dudes getting out of the car and coming into the building. I went to the door, which had a window—a misty window that you couldn't really see through, but you could see the silhouettes. These dudes were standing in the hall looking for my room. I heard one say, "Do you know which apartment he went into?" One was a soul cat and one was Italian. They were standing right in front of the door—all they had to do was push it. I was scared as hell.

Finally they left and drove away. I ran down to Jeanne Phillips' house. Ornette Coleman was there. I asked them, "Am I out of my nut? Is someone really trying to kill me?" Jeanne said, "Sunny, I'll tell you the truth, it could happen that way, because this music is bothering a lot of people who don't want black people to play this way. The whole club scene will come down if this music really happens." And Ornette said, "Yeah, that's what's happening, man." And I said, "Oh, shit, you shouldn't be saying this, you should be saying I was nuts or something." And he said, "Listen, those people paid me *not to play* for a whole year."

I stayed at Jeanne's until the sun came up.

Then, when I went to Europe with a group I co-led with Albert Ayler—that was the Free Jazz group, and Gary Peacock and Don Cherry was in it—a lot more strange things happened that I didn't understand. Like, when I had gone to Europe a year earlier with Cecil as the leader, everything had been pretty cool. But with Albert and me it was different.

Like, first of all, part of the tour was canceled when Albert hit some promoter in the mouth over ten dollars. I always thought he hit the wrong cat; the cats he should have hit, he was always smiling at. And like later, when we got ready to go home, I had to go to the embassy because I didn't have enough money. Everybody else in the band was cool. I didn't understand that shit—why was *I* the only one that was uptight? The embassy had to give me a transport ticket to go home. Another funny thing was like on the first tour, when I was playing with Cecil at the Montmartre in Copenhagen, one night this bartender went crazy. He started screaming and tore up the bar. "STOP THE MUSIC. I CANNOT STAND THE MUSIC." Then on *this* tour he comes back. Albert, who had played with us on the first tour, saw him and said, "There's that dude." And the dude came back, and he said, shaking hands and very quiet, "You have freed me." He'd been in a home for almost a year.

But a lot of strange things. In Denmark, Art Taylor, who's been living over there, told me we were chased to Europe by the business world. The tour was agreed upon by a lot of business cats just to get us out of the country. He said that anything could happen and to be careful. He said, "Look what happened to Eric Dolphy." I said, "Man, are you serious?" He said, "Just watch yourself." And I almost did get killed.

See, I was getting strange vibrations all the time we was in Europe. We were very in tune with the spirits when the Free Jazz group was over there—we were the most spiritual band in Europe at the time. Eric Dolphy, who had come over earlier with Mingus, had remained in Europe to play with us, with the Free Jazz group. He wanted to bust loose and really play free. But he died. Suddenly. Rumor was that he was poisoned. That set me off, and I began to realize that a lot of people were doing things to me to hang me up, and I started to get very nervous. It seemed like they was always doing something to me to stop me from the way I was playing. I was getting sick a lot—drugs being put in my drinks and shit like that. Then, when the time came to go home, everybody split on me—Albert said, "Bye," and flew home. I was stranded and frightened. I was in a hotel room alone in a foreign country. The embassy said, "O.K., we'll send you home on an army boat." They told me what boat to catch.

And this is how another attempt on my life came about. I had known a chick from the earlier tour, and she came up to me and invited me to stay at her home, which was sixty miles from Copenhagen. I said, "I'm catching the boat tomorrow and I can't go that far." She said, "Don't catch that boat, catch the next one." So I got a strange vibration, and I didn't go home with this lady. I packed my bags and headed for the train station to take a train to the port where the boat was.

When I got on the train, two cats got on right behind

me. They were dressed very debonair. They kept watching me. Smiling at me. Every time I went to eat, they followed me into the dining car—real foreign-intrigue shit! One time these dudes came and looked in my compartment and smiled and closed the door. I had some smoke, and I threw it out the window. I didn't know what was going on, and I took this little Swedish dagger out and kept it near me all the time. When we got to the port, to Bremerhaven, the dudes changed clothes, man, and they came out dressed like sailors—and they weren't no sailors. This really messed up my head, because what happened then was they changed into civvies again, and when I got off the train I saw the dudes cross the platform and get on a fucking train that was going *back!* It was too much, man. But that wasn't even it. On the boat, about three days at sea, a dude cuts into me, and he says, "You know the next boat that was leaving the day after this one? Everybody on that boat is just about dead, man." I said, "What happened?" He said, "There was an epidemic of spinal sclerosis or something. Somebody snuck a sick person on the boat, and he died on the boat —he would have been dead in a couple of hours anyway." They had taken about four people off the boat in helicopters. So I'm thinking, damn, if I'd went over to this broad's house and laid up an extra day in her crib and caught the other boat I'd be dead.

But then—it was weird—all these attempts on my life suddenly, strangely, just stopped. I've never been able to figure it out. I remember that it was around the time that J. C. Moses came into town and tried to play like me in the new system—and right after him Paul Motian. That made three New Jazz drummers. Right about then is when that shit broke up. Since around that time I ain't had no more hassles with people trying to kill me with violence. Since around that time I've been cool.

1965

The New Jazz and the Nature of Its Enemy

That much of the hostility to the New Jazz and New Jazz players is rooted in the deepest dreads inhabiting the contemporary American psyche has been made very clear by the position of many record producers, club owners, writers, white musicians (and yes, some Negroes too), who, like Leonard Feather, will name cold, cerebral European players like Attila Zoller and Denny Zeitlin to represent the avant-garde (the "healthy, affirmatively valid avant-garde," he called it), rather than Cecil Taylor or Ornette Coleman, Albert Ayler or Archie Shepp, and who, at the same time, reject as irrelevant any discussion in a music magazine of the racial (psychological, social, political) conditions which obtain in this country—who want to know why you don't just talk about the "aesthetics" of the music.

As though the value systems they live inside of could possibly allow for their recognition of, or engagement with, aesthetics; as though it were really beauty for which they called, and not murder, the murder of growth, in a people, in a music, in themselves; as though it were really aesthetics which they were interested in and not the uses they can make of the term to obfuscate some facts they would like to ignore; e.g., that very different social, historical, and psychological realities have decreed and controlled what the respective aesthetics of a Cecil Taylor and a Denny Zeitlin (or a Bill Evans) could be, and that the European-oriented criteria used to judge (and condemn) the aesthetics of the new Negro players are inapplicable.

These music lovers who refuse to acknowledge that the evolution of jazz is determined by Negroes, that jazz, and the changes within it, has always reflected where the Negro is, socially and psychologically; that the simultaneous rise of the New Jazz and Black Nationalism was not some weird coincidence; who will use words like "anti-jazz" or "nihilistic" or "lunatic yowlings and nursery babbles," to describe the music of the new Negro players, or say that what Cecil Taylor plays isn't jazz, are just telling us that they do not *want* what they hear to be jazz or to be real. They are enraged by the fact that the Negro is liberating himself from four hundred years of uncertainty regarding the worthiness of his identity, and that he has had the arrogance to not only demonstrate his liberation in his music, but to demand as well that his music be recognized as serious art and remunerated accordingly.

What these people are saying is that they do not want the order of their lives upset or altered, no matter how stifling and debilitating that order may be, because they dig it that way, because they are choosing to die. And to defend and sustain that condition, that limbo, to turn away the anxiety that is a symptom of an intuition of the possibility of growth in their lives, an intuition which the Negro's drive toward liberation from his own constricted order in America has unforgivably evoked in them and to which they lack the will and the courage to respond, they will, as LeRoi Jones has put it, "invent death for others"; will repress economically, physically, spiritually; will resort to, say, napalm, in certain not unrelated instances, if necessary.

What is America? Puerto Rican families in New York

now for several years no longer play their phonographs quite as loud as they used to; their women, going to work in the mornings, are not dressed so high and so colorfully anymore. That is America.

"There was," Norman Mailer says in his novel *The Deer Park*, "a law of life so cruel and so just, that one must grow or else pay more for remaining the same." But our society is committed to the destruction of growth.

An individual is only as mature as the emotional experiences he has entered and realized, as what he has allowed himself and been allowed to feel. And our society, having rejected feeling, is constructed so as to abort, in a complex of ways, most of our impulses toward genuine maturity. It is how much one can feel which ultimately determines the uses one will make of one's intelligence, talent, and energy. Our current state, however, does not reflect growth, but the evolution of an aberrated dichotomy between our intellect and our feelings and the deferral of our feelings to our intellect. Take, as an example, the remarkable scientific feat that is Telstar and the transoceanic communication with it of the Miss America Pageant. Or, even more frightening (because they are supposed to represent the opposite of this), the cold preoccupation of so many of our contemporary artists with conceptualization to the near exclusion of emotional content, as in much of our "new theater," which, because feeling is the only force that can give motion to ideas and the mechanisms of *genuine* change, can brilliantly reflect, but cannot transcend, our situation. Of course, the most hideous example is that while the discovery of atomic energy was indicative of man's fantastic technological achievement, the principal catalyst of the discovery was the "necessity" to make a bomb with it. The same men who could create the atom bomb were also capable of dropping it! Suicide and murder are all we can mean by atomic energy, in the way that suicide and murder (possessiveness) are all we can mean by love.

To deny the feelings is to enter insanity and disease.

Mailer has observed that shopping centers, a very characteristic artifact of our corporate civilization, viewed from the air at night, resemble cancer cells. Our external structures reflect our internal structures.

We have trapped ourselves inside a system (technological and moral) which, in the service of "comfort" and "security," insulates us from our mortality, and which, because there is creative impetus in the acute, sensuous awareness of physical vulnerability—in the necessity to challenge and overcome it—accomplishes precisely the opposite of its intention and implements and assures death. (*E.g.*, Muzak is piped into the elevators and halls of the American Cancer Society.) To obstruct emotional growth is the function of nearly all of our cultural institutions and customs—censorship, punishment, organized religion, corporate capitalism, et al., for they are antithetical to love, are about the evasion and restriction of experiences which might open the feelings and bring one closer to love. Love was the rejected energy that might have saved us, but instead of working toward its rediscovery, we have gone, and continue to go, in the reverse direction.

For instance, to compensate for the strength and ability to resist and combat disease, and to control the behavior of the body, a power which was there to be derived from love, what love could have enabled us to reach, we have substituted what are really synthetics of the love energy—vitamin pills, antibiotics, contraception, etc.—and which can be defined as necessary only by the lexicon of an insane society.

If, within the nature of our society, the contraceptive pill is nothing less than an urgent necessity, we must recognize that it is a necessity only because we have diverted our intelligence and energies away from an investigation into what our deepest needs and desires really are, and from developing the *emotional* technology to deal with them. Pregnancy is never an accident. It is determined by whatever desires, conscious or unconscious, positive or negative, constructive or destructive, are strongest, and to get in touch with and control our real desires is evaded and obstructed by contraception. The pill is finally about death, for it precludes the existential possibilities of the sex act, on the most basic of levels denies rather than implements freedom, and impedes the *need* of the human organism to exercise the natural and fundamental functions of self-determination and self-control, which keep it healthy and alive.

We make less and less possible any chance of escape from the predicament we are in with the cowardly uses to which we put our communications media and educational system, which encourage only conformity, banality, mediocrity, and which atrophy the sensibilities with a persistent and constant barrage of the bland, the sentimental, the inane, the untrue, the half-true; which have nothing to do with anything real.

The truth is shocking only because it is so unfamiliar. One can, for a month, watch television or read newspapers in America (which disseminate what we have chosen to regard as news, rather than what new poetry and music were created that day and which might reveal something of what our lives *could* be to us) or go to school in America for a year, and not be confronted with a single blatant or *impassioned* truth. And we choose not to trust the instincts of children who hate school.

Indeed, instead of trusting the instincts of our children, we destroy them with psychotic, paranoid warnings of danger, evil, perversion. And the motive is not misguided benevolence, but hatred, hatred for the child's vivaciousness and what he might discover about his mind and his body, about the true nature of his needs and how to satisfy them. Arrival at such discovery would promise a truly liberated state of being, but all of our insistence upon what is "normal," "real," "right," and "wrong," what is and what is not "possible," has only served to further alienate us from that state, to make it less accessible and more opaque to us.

We judge out of paranoia that human beings are evil (which actuality paranoia, generating its own reality, has created), and the purpose is to make sure that human beings will be nothing other than that, while the truth is that human beings will be whatever it is permitted them to be, whatever they are allowed to believe they can be and encouraged to be.

Growth can be achieved only through the genuinely benign validation of an impulse toward that end, never by punishment or censorship, which only hardens one into anger, the consequence of an aborted impulse, and leaves one there— catatonic or murderous. Thus we must come to terms with what we really mean by a "guidance" and "supervision" of a child that employs such methods, and of what this expresses about *our* lives and about our capability to give the child a true and sane perspective of the world and of himself.

When, in the name of love, we punish or censor a child, we communicate to him that a declaration of love is not the announcement of an unequivocal commitment by one person to the growth of another, but a promise not to grow. We "invent death" for the child on the pretext of shielding him from it (as insurance companies "invent death"), deliberately obscure the line between real and unreal danger, and rationalize an obligation to guide and supervise the child past the point where it has any real or healthy purpose, so as to accomplish the virtual imprisonment of his sensibilities and, concomitantly, reduce any challenge or threat to our own self-imposed and self-perpetuated emotional abjection.

A child has no recourse but to accept the position of his parents, about the world and about himself. To reject their word is to engender a wrath which he experiences as a very real and immediate threat to his survival. So it is made to be to the child's advantage, insofar as a livable relationship with his parents is concerned, *not to feel*, to dissociate himself from, and condemn, his healthiest impulses. And growth is halted at the point at which the experience which might have pushed it forward is denied. Moreover, because he is encouraged only to prove his parents right, the child is inclined to enter a forbidden experience for precisely that purpose—to deliberately (if unconsciously) fail at an endeavor, burn himself with matches, cross into the path of a car. . . . Indeed, the root of a problem that in adult life confronts many people is here, for it is not the fear of failing at an endeavor that frequently holds one back, but the fear of succeeding at it. Success implies change, *i.e.*, a transcendence of what has been parentally sanctioned, and failure does not.

A healthy, nonparanoid supervision—a supervision inspired by love—will most quickly free a child from the need of supervision. To love someone is to encourage his freedom, independence, self-reliance, and so, by this definition, it is considerably more difficult, psychically, and physically, to leave a home, an order, in which one has gone unloved, than a home in which one has experienced love. We are a society comprised of individuals who are largely unable to break with the narrow emotional orders into which we were born, and we help to enforce and perpetuate those orders in our "adult" lives with such macrocosmic extensions of our parents as police departments and censorship committees. But in sustaining and supporting such institutions we defeat what we claim is their purpose, because the first perversion is censorship itself and the greatest crime is the police, and both of these phenomena consequently *breed* "anti-social" behavior rather than forestall it. *All* "criminal acts"—even the most twisted and hideous of them—are, in their deepest, usually unconscious, motives, *political* acts, *revolutionary* acts, acts of rebellion against any of myriad forms of externally imposed authority whose dynamic has been a fear of life, not a love of it. Instead of dealing with this reality we choose to ignore it and to exist as helpless children, the point at which our growth was stopped. We relate to one another and react to new, positive forces which enter our lives, from that position. Ask a bum on the Bowery what system he would prefer, capitalism or socialism, and, for sure, he will name the former.

An emotional growth requires the ability to make perpetual new beginnings and psychic reconstructions, and the strength and courage to respond to our needs and adapt to new truths as they are revealed to us by our minds and our bodies. But unable (afraid) to feel deeply enough, we have only, no matter how different our "point of view," posture, manner of dress, etc., may be, re-created the emotional orders in which our fathers existed. The Catholic girl who becomes a prostitute has not abandoned Catholicism, but is carrying on a basic tenet of the faith—Thou Shalt Not Feel. The dilemma of the beatnik is not that he has rejected the values of his father, but that he has not rejected them enough. He continues to be directed by them, to be limited in the size and extent of what he can do—how much he can love and thus implement his philosophies—by them.

We speak of a "sexual revolution" in America, but at best we have assumed only the superficial mannerisms of one. It has not been an expanded consciousness of what is natural that has permitted us to function with what is ostensibly more freedom in sex, but simply that sex does not threaten the emotional order of our lives because there is no danger of love in it. And indeed, if certain forms of sexuality are still rejected as perverse, one must question whether it is the stigma of perversion one is rejecting—that one will become perverted—or the possibility of achieving some genuine form of contact with another human being which one has not been capable of experiencing within a conventional, sanctioned form.

The only real emotion that survives in America today is anger. And anger, when it does not result in suicide—catatonia and cancer; for the body receives the frustrations and rage created by the cowardice and ambivalence of the mind, and the cells rebel—results in murder, which is the instinctive attempt to exorcise from the body the "seeds" of that cancer, carried on an air heavy and toxic with the breath of our senators, clergymen, news commentators, corporation and advertising directors, etc. What Vietnam is about.

The most significant indication of the collapse of our culture that the conditions quickly outlined above have brought about may be found in our art. With the exception of the new energy in jazz, and a very few isolated individuals working in other forms, the bulk of contemporary American art is flatulent. At best it serves to chronicle our decline rather than to activate what might remain alive in its audience (to turn the anger in its audience to some *useful* energy and creative purpose), and thus assists in the perpetuation, not the destruction, of the cancer-ridden order in which we live. There are a great many talented people on the scene. But it is not about talent alone. Talent without emotion is meaningless.

The New Jazz is the one true remaining collective artistic energy in America which is communicating passion, emotional courage, and something like a celebration of life. This is why it is so despised. But if we succeed in killing our jazz musicians (the Negro), if we do not permit ourselves to dance to the musics of Taylor, Coleman, Shepp, Ayler, then the twist (DON'T TOUCH), or one of its variations, may be the last dance we do.

ALBERT AYLER
Photo by Charles Stewart

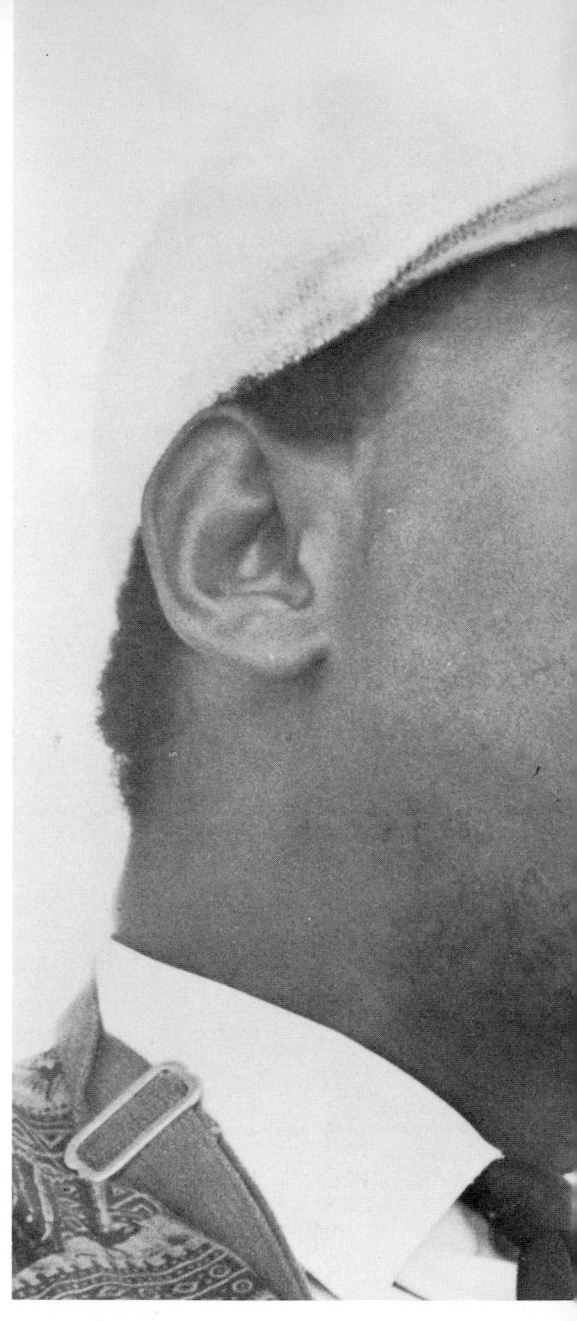

ARCHIE SHEPP
Photo by Joe Alper

CECIL TAYLOR
Photo by Charles Stewart

ANTHONY BRAXTON
Photo by Philippe Gras

SCOTT RICHARDS OF SRC
Photo by Magdalene Sinclair

UP
Photo by Magdalene Sinclair

MAURICE MC INTYRE
Courtesy Delmark Records

BOOKER LITTLE
Photo by Charles Stewart

STANLEY CROUCH
Courtesy of Flying Dutchman R

HORACE TAPSCOTT
Courtesy of Flying Dutchman R

SUN RA
Courtesy of Intergalactic Research

CHICK COREA
Courtesy of United Artists Records

MARION BROWN
Photo by Gail Anderson Brown

CHARLIE MINGUS
Photo by Joe Alper

SUNNY MURRAY

1970

The Emergence of
Jimmy Lyons

Since 1960, when he first began working with Cecil Taylor, alto-saxophonist Jimmy Lyons has been developing from a capable but diffident player into one of the more potent voices in the New Music. In recent appearances with Taylor and with Sunny Murray, Jimmy has been playing with a glowing assertiveness and often stunning beauty.

This past spring Jimmy's first album under his leadership (*Other Afternoons*, on the French Byg label, 529,309) was released, and it should make anyone who can get hold of it take serious notice—not only of his instrumental abilities, but also of his newly revealed and exceptional talent as a composer. The set is bristlingly alive and demonstrates Jimmy's capacity to play and write with startling and compelling rhythmic energy, a strong sense of melody, and a near-excruciating lyricism. He is accompanied on the record by three first-rate musicians: trumpeter Lester Bowie, who makes fierce and electric music; and two colleagues from Taylor's unit, Alan Silva, a fine bassist and brilliant cellist, and Andrew Cyrille, who has come to be one of the two or three heaviest drummers on the scene.

Born in Jersey City, December 1, 1933, Jimmy began playing alto when he was in high school. "At that time, and mostly from records, I was into Ernie Henry. I'd heard Bird first, but when I heard Ernie Henry I dug him more. Afterwards I heard Bird again and could see how *he* offered more. Then I started listening to people like Dexter Gordon, Wardell Gray, James Moody. . . . What really got me to start playing was a chick who lived next door. She had a baby grand and used to have people coming over and jamming all the time—Elmo Hope, Bud Powell, Thelonious Monk, and a lot of local players. I'd been playing for about six months then, mostly by myself, tunes like *Indiana*—I had no teacher, but I had a very good ear —and she heard me and one day she said, 'Hey, you're sounding good, why don't you come over?' I did, and Monk was there. We played for about a half-hour. He told me he wanted me to play a certain figure—sevenths—so I thought 'Sevenths?' I didn't know what he was talking about. I could hear it, but I'd never studied or learned. Monk said I was talented, but that I had to get down and take care of business; had to learn about music and do a lot of woodshedding. It was actually a beautiful experience. Later I played with Elmo Hope. We had a piano too at that time, and he used to practice on it afternoons when my mother was out working. We used to play and put things together, but I still hadn't had any formal training.

"In 1959 I met a cat named Rudy Rutherford. He wasn't as modern as some of the cats I was playing with, but he said, 'C'mon, I'll teach you how to play the saxophone.' I needed to learn, and he showed me a few things. He was very helpful.

"A year later I met Cecil. I was playing with a bass player at a club called Raphael's on Bleecker Street. Cecil worked opposite us on weekends. He had Archie Shepp and Dennis Charles with him, and the whole thing really knocked me out. Up until then I was playing mostly as a hobby, working at the Post Office, with just occasional gigs here and there. But hearing Cecil made me want to get into music full-time. Later a mutual friend said Cecil was looking for another horn, so I went down—he was living on Dey Street then—and we started rehearsing."

With Cecil, Jimmy was forced to take a leap from bebop into a whole new aesthetic and set of procedures. "I had to reorganize my whole approach to music and break a lot of habits. That's not very easy to do. I'd spent about a year trying to get myself together scale-wise and key-wise and tune-wise; then all of a sudden this other thing came up, and it took me a little while to get myself together in Cecil's music, to stop thinking chord-wise and to think about linking idea to idea. Like on the *Into the Hot* album, I didn't feel I was playing as well as I should be playing."

If Jimmy's work on *Into the Hot* (Impulse S-9) was uncertain and tentative (and still more imitative of Charlie Parker than an *extension* of the Parker tradition into the New Music, which in many ways it has since become), it gradually, as I have said, assumed authority and individuation. Witness the progression of his playing on Taylor's four succeeding albums: *Live at the Café Montmartre* (Fantasy 8604); *Nefertiti, The Beautiful One Has Come* (Fontana 888 609); *Unit Structures* (Blue Note 84237); and *Conquistador* (Blue Note 84260).

In my brief conversation with Jimmy I posed a number of questions at random. His comments on various aspects of his approach and aesthetic, as well as the New Music and the current scene in general, follow.

HIS INFLUENCES: "Well, of course there was Bird, and there is Cecil. Also I really dug Sonny Rollins a lot—and Jackie McLean. The man who wrote the liner notes for the Byg album said I had been influenced by Ornette, but I haven't really. I like Ornette, and I must say it's always good to hear him, but if Ornette and I sound alike in any way, it's because of the mutual influence we share of Bird. As for Bird, I think he was what every musician should be. He's an inspiration for every musician to do his own thing instead of being imitative. That's the realization I came to. I mean, the *major* thing to learn from Bird was not to play like him, but to play yourself."

HIS PROCEDURE: "Music has come to me to be an abstract thing. I don't try to imitate sounds like birds, or give a direct symbol of the sky or anything like that. I try to just let the music come out of myself without giving it any special meaning in front. I might think about what it might symbolize *after* I play it, but not before. It's more innate with me than deliberate."

THE NEW MUSIC VIS-À-VIS BEBOP: "Bebop was very romantic in a sense. It talked about heroic actions—things to do politically as well as musically, rather than *doing it now*. Of course, Bird got to some things, and a lot of the cats who are playing today aren't as modern as he was. When I say 'modern,' I mean using techniques that are indigenous to the modern school, like wide skips or things of that nature. But basically bebop was about the *idea* of doing what had to be done, rather than actually doing it. Now we're doing it."

THE MEANING OF FREEDOM: "When we talk about 'free' jazz it doesn't mean that you just play whatever pops into your head. It just means greater freedom of choice, and not being tied to some previous cat or things like chord structures."

THE JAZZ CONTINUUM: "To move to the next step, you have to have a knowledge of tradition—of the tradition of the black aesthetic—to have heard all of the things of the past and to truly have been moved by them. I don't mean just checking them out, but having been really *moved* by them."

ROCK: "Rock is dealing with a lot of electricity. You hear a full orchestra playing, then a rock group with four pieces comes along and blows them all away because of all that electricity. But I spent a year in North Carolina and heard a lot of those singers and players, and my father was a good dancer who had a good collection of blues records. I feel I've absorbed what most of rock is about, and the point now is to go on. I really want to push forward rather than dwell on what's gone before."

"CLASSICAL" ELECTRONIC MUSIC: "Much of it strikes me as bland. Of course, some of it would take a whole lot of fantastic blowing to get. But for me it lacks the human quality. When you hear a John Coltrane record, for example, you not only hear it, you visualize it too. I think the music of the black avant-garde is at least on the level of Stockhausen. But the black avant-garde doesn't have the kind of scene and patronage that he has. Those cats are able to work and write at their leisure."

FINDING A PLACE TO PLAY: "It's obvious by now that clubs are not the right atmosphere. You go to a club to hit on some chick, and the music comes along and pulls the whole thing apart. I prefer to play in schools or concert halls, because I think the intensity of the music demands the full attention."

FINDING AN AUDIENCE: "An audience will have to come through education. Black avant-garde music has to be inculcated into the ghetto, and schooling may accomplish that. I mean, if you go to a white slum neighborhood where people live in utter poverty and you play them a record by Chopin, they'll say, wow, that's really something. They may not really like it, they may be being hypocritical, but they'll have a certain respect for it because they've been educated that way. This is true of black slum neighborhoods too. There's no real respect for jazz, they haven't been taught in the schools that they should respect it. If it's taught in the school, they may not like it at first, but they will respect it and support it, and eventually they'll get to it."

I asked Jimmy about his plans for the future.

"Of all the groups out there playing, I think I'm most satisfied playing with Cecil. Of course, I'd also like to have my own context, to set up certain things and build up my own milieu. Like Coltrane. He was working out of his own thing, and he built it and built it and built it until it was overwhelming. In the last year and a half I've been doing a lot of composing—writing things down and putting them aside and developing them when I have the time. Often ideas pop up while I'm playing, and later I write them down. I'm also learning things from composing that are changing my playing. Writing and composing can be two very different things, of course. I've met a lot of cats who compose some out-of-sight shit, but they can't play it at all. I want to be able to do both well. What I'd really like would be, say, to write for three months, then wood-shed on it for six months, then play it in public for the next three months. Then I'd want to start fresh all over again with new material and ideas. Economics won't permit that, of course. But I want as best I can to keep moving from one area and context to another, to really get into one thing, get out of it, then get into another thing. I want to always be moving. Moving forward."

1966

Willis Jackson: Soul Night Live—or Dead?

Recently tenor saxophonist Willis "Gatortail" Jackson, who is well along into his thirties now, told an interviewer: "I have been stamped as a rocker and honker. There's no mystery about that. I had been blowing that way for years. But I'm a different man now. I've gotten away from that juvenile stuff. I've learned a few things."

A new Prestige release—*Soul Night Live* (7396)—demonstrates that Jackson's music has indeed changed. But after comparing this Jackson recording with those of an earlier vintage—mid- and late forties—one must disagree with the implication in his statement that he has *advanced* beyond his earlier way of playing; that is, one must disagree with the *definition* of growing up that is submitted with this recording.

Because while Jackson can claim, for his work on this album, a technical facility and a smoothness and polish absent in his earlier work, *Soul Night Live,* though it contains pleasant tunes and has a certain amiability, is finally a dull, bland, and blank record. There is no surprise in it, no energy, and no heat —not even the heat of the gymnast, let alone that of the lover. *Soul Night Live* is black Muzak—as tragic a phenomenon as is the Negro policeman.

No. Jackson has not grown beyond his earlier position; he has retreated from it.

".. . during the heyday of rhythm and blues," LeRoi Jones writes in *Blues People*, "blues-oriented instrumentalists, usually saxophone players, would vie to see who could screech, or moan, or shout the loudest and longest. . . . Men like 'Lockjaw' Davis, Illinois Jacquet, Willis 'Gatortail' Jackson, Big Jay McNeeley, Lynn Hope, and many others, would have 'honking' contests and try to outshout and outstomp any other saxophonist who would dare challenge them. Finally, when most of the 'honkers,' as they were called, had reached a similar competence, the contests got more athletic. Jay McNeeley used to lie on his back and stick his feet in the air while honking one loud screeching note or series of identical riffs. The riff itself was the basis for this kind of playing, the saxophonist repeating the riff much past any useful musical context, continuing it until he and the crowd were thoroughly exhausted physically and emotionally. The point, it seemed, was to spend oneself with as much attention as possible, and also to make the instruments sound as unmusical, or as *non-western*, as possible. It was almost as if the blues people were reacting against the softness and 'legitimacy' that had crept into black instrumental music since the advent of swing. . . . [While] one gets the idea that a man who falls down on his back screaming is doing so, more from a sense of performance than from any unalterable emotional requirement . . . the opposite idea also seems true—that for the Negro who found his most complete statement in rhythm and blues, the dramatic or *burlesqued* part of the performance might be as integral a part of the expression as the blues itself, since it made the departure, the separation, from the social implications of the white popular song complete."*

The rawness and the determinedly extreme and weird aural and physical devices and effects employed by the honkers were

* Le Roi Jones, *Blues People*, Morrow, 1963, pp. 172–73.

very purposeful. The honkers were rebelling against a grim irony, against at once the thievery and corruption of their identity, and the contempt in which their identity was held by the white man. If they strove to be, by all conventional *Western* standards, as "unmusical" as possible, and blatantly underscored what, from the white man's perspective, were the most despicable (read: frightening) characteristics of black sensuality, it was the only way left for them to preserve the purity— and honor—of their identity and to keep their identity safe from vitiating exploitation by the white sensibility. Because in spite of the fact that they knew themselves as Negroes to be despised, and had become half-convinced that they deserved to be, they still sensed as well that their identity as Negroes was worthy of preservation, that, indeed, it might be *more* worthy of its life (in its ability to feel life) than was the identity of the white man.

If bebop offered to other Negro musicians of the period a high art form with which not only to reassert, but also to *extend* the richness of the black identity and musical tradition, the honkers did not have the intellectual leverage to pursue that direction. But I think the honkers were, on their own terms, within reach of very great possibilities. If I find Willis Jackson's retreat from rebellion into banality lamentable (a retreat, it ought to be said, which he took in the company of all the aforementioned tenor players—listen to recent recordings by Eddie "Lockjaw" Davis, for example), it is because there was, in the kind of music he used to play, in the instincts that motivated and animated his stance, a vitality and a sexuality which, however onanistic in its heats and "limited" in its aesthetics, gave hint that some other end was within his potential. I mean, there was *feeling* in his music. If the primary property of that feeling was anger, it was at least an anger which gave motion, *i.e.*, life, to his music; a *kinetic* anger as differentiated from the *catatonic* anger that has produced an album like *Soul Night Live*. (The reason the honkers were largely ignored or censured, not only by white audiences but also by the Negro middle class—even that faction of the Negro middle class that could find it within itself to accept bebop—was not because of the aesthetic "limitations" of their music but because of its extraordinary emotive quality. The middle-class sensibility, black or white, certainly does not eschew mediocrity.)

Of course, anger which animates and anger which paralyzes and numbs are only a nuance of mood apart, and the former will frequently dissolve into the latter, for anger, in its fevers, can evaporate the blood. Thus it could be said of the honkers that their anger—as manifested in their "excesses"—was ultimately self-defeating, that it enervated the blood of their music and so stopped their music from evolving into any kind of truly "creative" expression; that their anger transformed, inevitably, into listlessness, rather than passion. Rebellion, it could be argued, must function finally as the means toward a new end, and the honkers, so angry as to be blinded by anger, could not find that new end, could not take that riff anywhere, and so were left to repeat it into oblivion.

That *could* be said, and that *could* be true. But perhaps something else is more true. Perhaps the size of the honker's courage was not equal to the size of his anger, and that the absence of a strong enough trust and conviction in the *legitimacy* of his anger, not the anger itself, is what defeated him. Perhaps he could not allow himself to be angry enough. Those forces in the world which externally operated to limit the size and scope of his reality and possibilities, and which had given cause to his rebellion, had also come, through years of conditioning and inculcation, to have their internal counterpart—the ultimate objective of the "program"—and perhaps it was that in the pit of his psyche, the possibility that he deserved to be despised came to outweigh and to be more real to him than the possibility that he did not, and that it was the cruel proportions of this ambivalence which weakened the outward thrust of his anger, turned his anger further inward, dissolved it into a heat which burned and blunted his nerve endings and rendered it incapable of propelling him beyond rebellion and into real growth.

There was risk in taking the position which the early Willis Jackson took, and there was courage in his stance— enough courage to enter extremes and to travel a certain distance away from an ignoble, cancerous acquiescence to the reality he had inherited. But his courage was finally not great enough to take him what were perhaps only a few, but crucial, steps further along. He was able to achieve an orbit around, but unable to totally loose and liberate himself from, that force which he was rebelling against, because his ambivalence broke the rhythm and momentum of his charge and would not permit him to be sure that he did, after all, have the *right* to break away. So Jackson came down and back with nothing to tell about the stars except, *e.g.*, *Soul Night Live*, that it is futile— or "juvenile"—to attempt to reach them.

What I am suggesting is that "the saxophonist repeating the riff much past any useful musical context, continuing it until he . . . was thoroughly exhausted physically and emotionally," had he dared to challenge that inner voice which warned him that he had reached his limits, and dared to play that riff another time, one more time, might have entered a *new* context; might have been rejuvenated, might have come upon a new surge of energy with a thrust sufficient to the task of lifting him over the hump of his exhaustion and propelling him into a new reality, a reality that might have been waiting on the other side of his exhaustion. (Say, the reality which Albert Ayler got to.) Somewhere in his body Jackson must have recognized that possibility. But he allowed the negative half of his ambivalence to control and determine his course.

Indeed, it must have seemed to him more than difficult not to (next door to impossible), for as he entered the extremes and the anxiety which accompanied them—an anxiety threatening, in its fevers, disease, madness, death—the battle between the impulses which urged him on and the force which called him back may have been so fierce as to seem to enervate his will and his body past the point where they could be rescued by courage. For Jackson to go on then was to risk death, certainly to risk what we mean by insanity. And yet to take precisely that risk may have been necessary to the survival of his "soul" and to the continuation of his growth. But Jackson did not take that final risk. He went the opposite direction, and he arrived at what we mean by maturity.

1971

An Interview with Booker Little*

Booker Little, twenty-three-year-old composer, arranger, and trumpet player (the order is arbitrary, each role has equal importance to him), has lately come to demonstrate, in recordings and as musical director of the Max Roach group, a talent that promises size.

As is true of many jazz players of his generation, Booker is a product of the conservatory. He has found that experience to be "invaluable," but has discovered that it can tend to bind one to conventional precepts and result in an excessive emphasis on the *technical* aspects of making music—at the cost of the *emotional* aspects.

"My background has been conventional," he says, "and maybe because of that I haven't really become a leftist, though my ideas and tastes now might run left to a certain degree. I think the emotional aspect of music is the most important. A lot of guys, and I've been guilty of this too, put too much stress on the technical, and that's not hard to do when you've learned how to play in school. I think this goes along with why a lot of

*This piece was originally printed in *Metronome* in 1961 and reprinted in *Jazz & Pop* in 1971.

trumpet players have come up lately sounding one way—like Clifford Brown. They say everyone's imitating him now, and that's true in a way, and in a way it isn't. Clifford was a flashy trumpet player who articulated very well. He started a kind of trumpet playing that's partly an outgrowth of Fats Navarro— insofar as having a big sound, articulating well all over the instrument, and having an even sound from top to bottom. Most of the younger guys, like myself, who started playing in school, they'd have the instructor driving at them, 'Okay, you gotta have a big sound, you gotta have this and that.' Consequently, if they came in sounding like Miles, which is beautiful for jazz, they flunked the lessons. They turned toward someone else then, like Clifford. Donald Byrd is a schooled trumpet player, and though he's away from that now, he'll never really be able to throw it out of his mind."

Booker was born into a musical family in Memphis, Tennessee, on April 2, 1938. His father was a trombonist in a Baptist church band, and his mother was a church organist; an older sister sang for a time with the London Opera Company. Booker began playing trumpet in his high-school "classical" and marching band. "At first I was interested in the clarinet, but the instructor felt trumpet would be best—because he needed trumpet players. Jazz records were very scarce in Memphis at that time, but there were a lot of guys who were interested in it. George Coleman was one. He was probably one of the most progressive people around town at the time, and there was also Louis Smith, who is my cousin. They were listening. I was rather close to George, because he was in the same high school. He was sharp enough to take things off records. I was fourteen or fifteen then, and he sort of got me started. I played with some groups around town, and then when I graduated I went to the Chicago Conservatory. Being in Chicago gave me greater exposure to things, because guys were always coming through."

At the conservatory Booker majored in trumpet and minored in piano. He also studied theory, composition, and orchestration. In his third year, when he was nineteen, he met Max Roach through Sonny Rollins, and soon afterwards Roach called him for a record date. About that time he decided to quit school. "I gave it up because I realized there wasn't much I could do as far as being a 'classical' musician, which my parents had wanted, was concerned." The record date eventually resulted in a regular working association with the Roach quintet that continued through 1958, when Booker took a leave of absence to free-lance in New York. During that period he worked and/or recorded with (among others) John Coltrane, Sonny Stitt, Slide Hampton, Ed Shaugnessy, Teddy Charles, Mal Waldron, and Abbey Lincoln. He also recorded an album for United Artists and another for Time. In early 1960 he rejoined Roach as musical director of the group.

Of late, however, Booker has come to look ahead to the possibility of forming his own group. The repertoire would consist primarily of his own compositions.

"I think I've found the way I want to play on my instrument, and now I want to concentrate on the sound I'd like to build around it." Currently Booker has a working agreement with Candid Records, for whom he has already made an album (with Eric Dolphy) comprised entirely of his own writing. At the time we spoke, he was working on the orchestrations for an album that is to feature Coleman Hawkins "in a modern setting."

"I don't think there's very much of my work prior to these Candid dates that expresses how I feel now about what I want to do."

What Booker wants to accomplish as a composer involves drawing on his knowledge of what he terms "the legitimate aspects of writing" without permitting himself to be confined by them.

"Those who have no idea about how 'classical' music is constructed are definitely at a loss—it's a definite foundation. I don't think it should be carried to a point where you have to say this is this kind of phrase and this is that kind of development. Deep in your mind, though, you should maintain these thoughts and not just throw a phrase in without it answering itself or leading to something else. Say, I know the chord I want the piano player to play and I give it to him. But the other instruments won't necessarily be playing that chord. Most of the guys who are thinking completely conventionally— they'd say, 'well, maybe you've got a wrong note in there.' But I can't think in terms of wrong notes—in fact, I don't hear any notes as being wrong. It's a matter of knowing how to integrate the notes and, if you must, how to resolve them. Because if you insist that this note or that note is wrong, I think you're thinking completely conventionally—technically— and forgetting about emotion. And I don't think anyone would deny that more emotion can be reached and expressed outside of the conventional diatonic way of playing, which consists of whole steps and half-steps. There's more emotion that can be expressed by the notes that are played flat. Say, it's a B flat, but you play it flat and it's not an A and it's not a B flat, it's between them, and in places you can employ that, and I think it has great value. Or, say, the clash of a B natural against a B flat.

"I'm interested in putting sounds against sounds, and I'm interested in freedom also. But I have respect for form. I think solo sections of a piece can sometimes be played, say, on a basic undersound, which doesn't necessarily tell the soloist how many choruses to take. You say, 'You blow awhile. You try and build your story and resolve it.' One thing I wrote for [supervisor] Nat Hentoff on the Candid date is like that completely. The undervoices were playing a motif, and I just improvised on the sound. It had a definite mood, and the mood didn't warrant my running all over the trumpet.

"There are a lot of people who think the new direction should be to abolish form, and others who feel that it should be to unite 'classical' forms with jazz. The relationship between 'classical' and jazz is close, but I don't think you have to employ a 'classical' technique as such to get something that jells. I

think the main reason a lot of people are going into it is because jazz hasn't developed as far as composition is concerned.
It's usually a twelve-bar written segment, and then everybody
goes for themselves. Personally, I don't think it's necessary to
do either of these things to really accomplish something different and new. And I think sometimes a conscious effort to do
something different and new isn't as good as a natural effort.

"In my own work I'm particularly interested in the possibilities of dissonance. If it's a consonant sound, it's going to
sound smaller. The more dissonance, the bigger the sound. It
sounds like more horns; in fact, you can't always tell how many
there are. And your shadings can be more varied. Dissonance is
a tool to achieve these things."

Booker has been impressed by the writing of Charlie
Mingus. "He's been thinking rhythmically, in terms of breaking
up rhythms, and that interests me. He's definitely a giant as
far as writing is concerned. He stems from another giant, Duke
Ellington. Duke is one of my favorite writers. He's a man who's
worked at a sound and never wavered, and his musical person-
ality is always identifiable as his. Slide Hampton has impressed
me when he's writing for no other reason than himself. He has
a terrific mind. And I thought the Gunther Schuller Atlantic
date with Ornette Coleman had some terrific writing."

As a trumpet player Booker concedes that his major influence, much for the reasons stated earlier in this piece, has been
Clifford Brown. "Yes, to a degree I'm afraid there was an influence, but I do think I've rid myself of it. I remember when
I was living at the YMCA in Chicago. Sonny Rollins was living
there too. You had to go down to the basement to practice,
and once he heard me listening to a Clifford Brown record. I
was playing it over and over again, and I guess I was driving
him mad, because he was trying to practice himself. He asked
me what I was doing, and I told him I was trying to learn the
melody. He told me that it was probably best that I go buy a
sheet on it, because if I kept listening to the way he played it,
it was going to rub off, and I was going to play it the same way.

I never forgot what he said, though I did continue listening to Clifford Brown records. Brownie was the easiest guy for me to really get close to, as far as finding out what was going on. I like the way he played his lines."

Booker is very concerned with remaining within the mood of a piece when he solos.

"Jazz soloing, as a result of the methods Bird introduced, started a very involved technique, and Bird and some of the others reached a very high degree of emotion, higher than most of the soloists to follow. Sonny Rollins has reached the same height, probably because he was around to hear them. He not only heard them say this is an A major or a D seventh, he also heard, firsthand, what they did with it—the kind of emotion they got out of it. A guy learning as I learned—say, the first chord in the bridge is an A-minor seventh—well, the first thing he had to do was figure out every note in the A-minor seventh, and when it came to playing it, he had to make sure he hit all the right notes. I think this is important, but not half as important as concentrating on staying within the mood. Say, you're playing *Blue Monday*. I don't think it's saying very much for you if you start to play it and then just rip and run all over the instrument. But again, you can get so involved with the technical aspect of playing that you do that—it's not hard for that to happen. Miles Davis minimized how much trumpet playing you could do as much as anybody could minimize it. But many people have a misconception about him. They say he can't play trumpet. But he's a fantastic trumpet player with a fantastic mind. He was one of the first guys around who didn't have to play every note in an A-minor chord to give you the impression of an A-minor chord and to get the mood that the section needed. There's so many areas of trumpet playing that can be employed, and they don't have a lot to do with the 'legitimate' end of trumpet playing as such. There are a lot of notes between notes—they call them quarter-tones. They're not really quarter-tones, but notes that are above and below the 440 notes. This is something Miles employs a lot, and I doubt if he even thinks about it."

As a result of the influence Clifford Brown has exerted on
the younger trumpet players, Booker said he believes there is
a serious need for everyone to break away and find his individu-
ality.

"The problem isn't only with trumpet players, and that's
why I think it's very good that Ornette Coleman and some
other people have come on the scene. Ornette has his own ideas
about what makes what, and I don't think it's proper to put
him down. I do think its okay to talk about what his music has
and what it doesn't have. I have more conventional ideas about
what makes what than he does, but I think I understand clearly
what he's doing, and it's good. It's an honest effort. It's like a
guy who puts sponges on his feet, steps in paint, and then
smears it on the canvas. If he really feels it that way, that's it.
At one end you have a guy who does it from a purely intellectual aspect, and at the other a guy who does it from a purely
emotional aspect. Sometimes both arrive at the same thing. I
think Bird was more intellectual in his playing than Ornette
is. I think Ornette puts down whatever he feels. But I think
both ways have worth, though I don't believe Ornette himself
has the worth of a Charlie Parker. Bird consumed everything,
all that had been before him, and then advanced it all, and I
don't think Ornette has consumed everything, though I'm sure
he's heard it. I do think that what Ornette's doing is part of
what jazz will become.

"You know, there are so many things to get to. Most people who don't listen often say jazz is a continuous pounding,
and this is something I can feel too. I think there are many
emotions that can't be expressed with that going on. There are
certain feelings that you might want to express that you could
express better if you didn't have that beat. Up until now, if
you wanted to express a sad or a moody feeling, you would
play the blues. But it can be done in other ways."

Booker is concerning himself with exploring some of the
"other ways." If his aesthetic remains bound to the conventional precepts in which his education is rooted, he is trying
to find out how to make his conservatory education nourish

rather than taint or restrain his music. His most recent work both in person and on records is evidence of his certainly growing skill and courage as a composer and an instrumentalist who is likely going to achieve real stature.

[Booker died of uremia in 1961, just a few months after this interview was originally printed. It is, of course, impossible to know what changes would have occurred in his music and philosophy over the ensuing decade had he lived. But the position he was in at the time of his death in relation to the position of Ornette Coleman and Cecil Taylor is representative, I think, of an interesting syndrome, a syndrome with which I attempt to deal in the following piece. R.L.]

1969

Reform Is Reactionary: A Review of *The Quest**

> Bebop was very romantic in a sense.
> It talked about heroic actions, things
> to do politically as well as musically,
> rather than *doing it now* . . . basically
> bebop was about the *idea* of doing what
> had to be done, rather than actually
> doing it. Now we're doing it.
> —Jimmy Lyons

By the late 1950's most jazz musicians had arrived at the conclusion that bebop (one of the most important systems in the history of music, and the dominant system in jazz for nearly two decades) was becoming obsolete.

For some musicians (already in the hills and preparing to march on the capitol) the solution to the problem of where to

* ERIC DOLPHY AND BOOKER ERVIN WITH MAL WALDRON. *The Quest* (Prestige 7579): Eric Dolphy (as, cl); Booker Ervin (ts); Mal Waldron (p); Ron Carter (cl o); Joe Benjamin (b); Charlie Persip (d). *Status Seeking; Duquility; Thirteen; We Diddit; Warm Canto; Warp & Woof; Fire Waltz.*

go and how to proceed was, clearly, to abandon the bebop system. These men recognized (and they were in possession of the leverage and the courage to act upon the recognition) that to make music which was expressive of an emergent new ethos, and relevant to the new imperatives—that could embody and reflect the tensions, dangers, revelations, and liberated energies of the times—it was necessary to jettison the predetermined and consequently circumscribing) bebop structure, and to re-create an environment that was conducive to the existential growth of their music, an environment in which there were no antiquated and/or preimposed standards, disciplines, etc., to obstruct, subvert, and limit the realization of the new possibilities they envisioned. They were not in terror of letting go, of the prospect of dislocation and chaos. They understood that ultimately, *out* of what they played, *as* they played, a new and transcendent order, organic and viable, would *naturally* emerge and develop.

For other musicians, however, such a drastic measure was not feasible. It was just not feasible. Their consciousness and sensibilities were locked not only into bebop's strictly musical precepts, but also into the social, political, and emotional order out of which bebop came. To break with those precepts was to break with that order, and that was impossible. If bebop, as black consciousness evolved, had become increasingly imprisoning, its familiar and time-honored conventions also constituted a safe place to be, a security which they could not bring themselves to gamble.

For these musicians, the alternative to what Cecil Taylor and Ornette Coleman proposed—the "responsible" alternative ("complete freedom is not the answer," one musician could say)—was to "reform" the bebop order; that is, to try to keep bebop and to try to make it continuingly viable, by attempting to revitalize and enlarge its material and emotional content and references. This kind of endeavor (which to the degree that cool and progressive jazz were examples of it, actually began as far back as the late forties in the *anticipation* of the radical vision of the revolutionaries) was pursued, at the one pole, by incorporating elements of other forms, such as European symphonic concepts, and, at the other, by "returning to the roots." But the musics created on this basis resulted in little more than genres (*e.g.*, funky/hard bop, third stream) and inevitably amounted to regressions or aberrations. Hard bop was archly self- (soul-) conscious, affected, and emotionally strained. Third stream, which attempted to marry two antithetical traditions, provided, with its stillborn plastic progeny, some heavy evidence for the dangers of miscegenation.

Of course, just as bebop in its nascent stages had, in part, been a reaction against the "legitimization" of black music during the swing era, the funky school was, in many ways, a reaction against the "whitened," Westernized (*i.e.*, antispiritual) nature of cool and progressive jazz, and served to assert for black musicians the existence and richness of their tradition. But the funky school and the third stream both existed, each in its way (the hip rationalizations, in the former case, of "purification" or "regrouping forces" notwithstanding) as means with which to stall and to avoid taking the leap forward—the leap from, if you will, the sentiment of freedom to the actualization of it. A reconnection with, and reaffirmation of, the essences of the black/spiritual musical tradition was indeed necessary at the time, but it did not require a backward turn, as the work of Ornette Coleman, out of whose liberated procedures jazz essences naturally resurfaced, and with a powerful contemporaneity, ought to make very clear.

The recently reissued *The Quest*, recorded and originally released in 1961, includes elements of both the hard-bop and third-stream idioms. It also includes elements of the New Music, but rather than follow those elements into the new reality which they represent, the music in *The Quest* subsumes them into the bebop context. As its title implies, *The Quest* is after a way out of the predicament of bebop. But since it does not let go of bebop, it results, ultimately, in a dead end; that is to say, an "experimental" music, a music that is devoid of *genuine* risk and, hence, the vital substances of discovery and surprise—though, for sure, sufficiently hip in its pretensions to seduce and indulge "progressively" inclined sensibilities. Liberal music.

Indeed, an analogy which may serve to clarify the position of this album at the time of its recording, vis-à-vis the New Music, would be the difference between Martin Luther King (*The Quest*) and Malcolm X (the New Music).

All of the compositions, for example (by Mal Waldron, who was credited as the leader on the original edition), can be said to claim an immediately engaging grace and swing. *Warm Canto* and *Duquility* are, one might say, exceptionally pretty ballads, and the liberties with (variously) harmony, meter, and melodic construction which are taken in *Status Seeking, We Diddit, Thirteen, Warp & Woof,* and *Fire Waltz* may be described as intelligent, imaginative, and even, upon occasion, bold. And these numbers are performed by a very capable group of musicians who play with what could be defined as heat, strength, and emotional abandon.

But the definitions and values of these favorable comments —the criteria upon which these comments are based—are those of the bebop lexicon and aesthetic circa 1954. By the standards and interpretations of 1961, and the "free" system of the revolutionaries *which was already emergent,* to apply such terms as "emotional abandon" and "bold" to the music in *The Quest* is to vitiate language. Furthermore, it is to obfuscate the achievement of the New Music, which, in its total departure from many long-enduring properties and formats in jazz, and in its expression of a radically new consciousness and sensibility, was *truly* bold and emotionally unbound. A new dynamic was abroad, and qualities in bebop which were once profound and beautiful had become, in comparison to the depths of emotion and spirit which the revolutionaries had reached, shallow and imprisoning. And the bebop order, as has already been suggested, was terminal anyway—the level of social, political, and emotional consciousness which had informed and defined it had been transcended. No amount of renovation or modernization, no matter how "intelligent" or "imaginative," could, in the long run, rescue and sustain it as a relevant and viable medium, because its very infrastructure was in decay. Indeed, such attempts at "reform" of the bebop order as *The Quest* represents could only serve to *forestall the entrenchment of the new, revolutionary aesthetic.*

The most compelling moments on the LP are supplied, predictably enough, by the late Eric Dolphy. But Dolphy was the perfect example of a musician who, while comprehending the validity of what the revolutionaries proposed, was unable to *completely* sever himself from the bebop syndrome. Dolphy was acutely aware of the limitations of bebop, but he was never able to bring himself to make the run from the one reality to the other. Even his most adventurous work was barely more than a reconnaissance into the existential abyss of the new "free" music—there was nearly always slack in the umbilical cord—and he frequently confined himself to working within contexts, such as this one, where he would be surrounded by strong, stabilizing, bop forces. His solo on the opening track, *Status Seeking,* provides a pointed example.

Who could swear that it was not the tension of his ambivalence, the agonizing choice that was left for Dolphy to make, which brought on his early death? The posthumous lauding of Dolphy (who was, to be sure, a brilliant musician) has been due in no small measure to the fact that so many people can identify with his kind of predicament.

Dolphy and Waldron's "quest" in this set for a viable music was self-defeatingly anchored in an obsolete order that could not, by the 1960's, provide the dynamic for a music of true urgency, challenge, and adventure. *The Quest* is ultimately a depressing record. It was well-crafted, but it took neither the musicians nor the audience to any place they had not been before.

1969/70

Two Brief Reviews*

The Jazz Excursion into "Hair," by Bobby Bryant

The fact that *Hair* is a jive show, a show designed by, and for, tourists; and the fact that the songs from *Hair* are shallow and sentimental, does not necessarily preclude the possibility of a jazz musician making exceptional music from the score. (Among the literally thousands of transcendent jazz interpretations of inferior material, listen to, say, Billie Holiday's rendition of the psychotic *Don't Explain,* or Cecil Taylor playing the supermaudlin *This Nearly Was Mine.*)

But trumpeter-flugelhornist Bobby Bryant, and Shorty Rogers, who wrote the arrangements, are no more musicians than the people responsible for *Hair* are musicians, writers, or directors. They are businessmen. And this album, in which they

*BOBBY BRYANT. *The Jazz Excursion into Hair* (Pacific Jazz 20159).

MODERN JAZZ QUARTET. *Space* (Apple STAO 3306): John Lewis (p); Milt Jackson (vb); Percy Heath (b); Connie Kay (d). *Visitor from Venus; Visitor from Mars; Here's That Rainy Day; Dilemma; Adagio from Concierto de Aranjuez.*

have apparently set out to exploit the Herb Alpert vogue, and every commercial possibility inherent in mediocrity, sounds as though a board meeting rather than a rehearsal preceded the recording session.

While it might seem sufficient to say that the score of *Hair* gets the reading it deserves with this album, I think records like this need to be destroyed, not simply dismissed, because they work to certify, for the uninformed, that jazz is dead, when jazz, in its honest, uncorrupted manifestations, has never been more vital.

Space, by the Modern Jazz Quartet

Permit me to submit a "found" critique.

"They wouldn't have rock or avant-garde jazz at the White House. If they did, they would all think they were being attacked. All of a sudden a rock or an avant-garde jazz musician jumps up and goes into his thing, and these people would run and hide under tables, because all their guilt would scare hell out of them. . . . If the musician is playing like a rock or an avant-garde jazz musician does, then what are the people acting like? . . . Now, if Lawrence Welk plays there—doo-pee-doo— oh, they cool now, man. *The submission in the music tells them that the people is submissioned.*"

—Sunny Murray, *JAZZ & POP*, April/May 1969

"His Imperial Majesty represents a dynasty over 2,500 years old and a civilization over 6,500 years old. He has graciously consented to be entertained by the best of our civilization—American jazz, as it is so ably represented by the Modern Jazz Quartet—or as we 'in' people call them, the MJQ."

—President Richard Nixon, speaking at a White House reception for the Shah of Iran, fall, 1969.

1970

Introducing
Anthony Braxton

To anyone still questioning the validity of the aesthetic and systems at which Cecil Taylor, Ornette Coleman, and John Coltrane arrived, I would first of all recommend that he listen more attentively to the work of these men. But I would also suggest that he make it a point to hear the very strong and very exciting music(s) of an emergent collection of jazz players from Chicago who constitute what is already a third generation of New Music players (Ayler, Murray, Shepp, etc., representing the second), and whose very existence should certify beyond dispute the substance and viability—and irrevocability—of the innovations which Taylor, Coleman, and Coltrane forged.

Anthony Braxton, Maurice McIntyre, Joseph Jarman, Lester Bowie, Roscoe Mitchell, Richard Abrams, Malachi Favors, LeRoy Jenkins, Leo Smith, Steve McCall, and Henry Threadgill are just some of the gifted and mostly very young musicians involved in the Chicago movement. These men have not only passionately embraced the new aesthetic, but they are adding dimensions to it that were likely undreamed of by their precursors. In addition to the utilization of extraordinary instruments like harmonicas, accordions, sirens, Chinese gongs, Hawaiian tiples, rattles, whistles, etc., the Chicago players are into using objects like garbage-can covers, chairs, and beads to make sounds with. They are also incorporating theatrical and visual effects with very provocative results.

Although I had heard most of the Delmark albums (the Chicago label which has recorded many of these players), my first live exposure to the music being produced by the Chicago movement came one evening last May when a five-man cooperative group called the Creative Construction Company of Chicago played its first New York concert at the Peace Church in Greenwich Village.

The music which Anthony Braxton, LeRoy Jenkins, Leo Smith, Richard Abrams, Steve McCall, and Richard Davis made that evening was lifting and invigorating, full of movement, wit, adventure, and surprise. It reminded me in its spirit as well as its setting of the loft and coffeehouse gigs that Archie Shepp, Bill Dixon, Albert Ayler, Marion Brown, Don Cherry, Pharaoh Sanders, et al., used to make some seven or eight years ago—when they were still playing out of the first waves of the black energy eruption. The music was as new and as fresh, and the same kind of joy exuded from the musicians, as though each sound they made represented for them a new discovery about music and about themselves, and each discovery surely had millennial proportions.

Especially impressed by Anthony Braxton, I introduced myself to him at the completion of the concert and invited him to be interviewed. We got together to talk several days later.

Braxton was born on Chicago's Southside and turned twenty-five this past June. He is "classically" trained—he studied for a few years with private teachers and at the Chicago School of Music—and has composed orchestral pieces and piano music. Although the alto saxophone is his chief instrument, he plays all the woodwinds, some brass, and various other conventional, semiconventional, and unconventional instruments. The first jazz group he ever heard was the Dave Brubeck quartet. "That was at a very early age. I didn't dig Brubeck very much, but I was attracted to Paul Desmond. Actually, it was after listening to Desmond, whom I heard way before Charlie Parker, that I decided to play woodwinds. He was very important to me, and he's still one of my favorite musicians."

In 1961 Braxton heard Ornette Coleman's *The Shape of Jazz to Come*. "I had gone by a friend of mine's house, his father listened to jazz, and he said, 'Listen to this, because this is what's going to be happening, this is where the music will be going.' When I heard Ornette, I was immediately affected by him. I was afraid of him, because he was so different in relation to what I'd been hearing. I was very conscious of the fact that something was happening with this music—it drew me very strongly, and I knew that someday I would have to deal with it."

Braxton continued, for several more years, to play with his "Desmond sound" and to listen, in addition to Duke Ellington, Miles Davis, and Charlie Parker, to people like Lee Konitz and Warne Marsh, "whom I still love. I have every record Lee Konitz and Warne Marsh ever made. Konitz, even by today's standards, was into some far-out things—*Marshmallow, Ice Cream Konitz.* . . ." Later Braxton encountered Roscoe Mitchell and Joseph Jarman. "Those guys really turned my head around. They were so advanced even then it was incredible. I thought I had some knowledge of music, but I found I didn't know anything."

In 1963 Braxton went into the Army, spending most of his hitch in Korea. When he got out in 1966 he met again with Jarman and Mitchell, who were by then involved with the Association for the Advancement of Creative Musicians, the cooperative of some thirty or forty musicians that is nearly four years old now and from which the Chicago movement has stemmed. He began then to really get into Ornette, and Eric Dolphy and John Coltrane, and to "stop playing like Paul

Desmond." He also, during this period, got seriously turned on to "classical" music.

"One day I happened to put an Arnold Schoenberg record on by accident, and almost passed out. And so there was something else for me to check out. I was very much affected by Schoenberg, and he led me to people like Berg and Webern and Stockhausen, and finally to John Cage."

Braxton was playing concerts with other AACM musicians by this time, and he also recorded two albums for Delmark— *3 Compositions of New Jazz* (DS-415) and a two-record set of alto solos which (held up for various, mysterious, reasons) was scheduled for release in late 1970. He also played on Richard Abrams' *Levels and Degrees of Light* (DS-413).

In 1969 Braxton went to Europe with LeRoy Jenkins, Leo Smith, and Steve McCall. He spent nearly a year there, working all over and recording two albums for Byg and Polydor. Only one set is in release (Byg 529,315). He also made an album under Alan Silva's leadership for Byg, *Luna Surface* (529,312). While in Paris Braxton met Ornette Coleman, who heard him play and invited him to come to New York. Braxton responded to the invitation and, with LeRoy Jenkins, came here early this spring and stayed with Ornette until he was able to get located. Of Ornette, Braxton says, "I've always loved him, loved and respected his music. And after getting a chance to meet and know him, I'm thoroughly in awe of him, the kind of person he is. He's been such a good friend. He has my deepest respect, musically and personally."

Despite Ornette's hospitality, the aforementioned concert, a gig and record date with Chick Corea, and a record date with Marion Brown, Braxton had not had an easy time of it in New York, though no worse a time than most New York musicians. During our talk he told me he was looking for a day job. He had recently applied for a job as a stock boy and had been turned down.

We talked about the economic aspects of the scene, and then Braxton began to discuss his own music, and the properties, characteristics, and directions of the Chicago movement in general.

"When I got out of the Army I joined the AACM and found everybody deep into exploring different avenues. Roscoe Mitchell talked of colors. Steve McCall was into shadings—he knows more about shadings, I think, than any other percussionist. Joseph Jarman, at the time, was into theater, and getting politically involved; he was very concerned about the social aspects of what was happening in this country. Henry Threadgill was talking about healing through his music, and he was learning about different sounds and how those sounds affected people—like the relationship of one note to a particular illness. Richard Abrams was concerned with the spiritual aspects of music. So many different things were, and are, happening. If you talked to Leo Smith, he would talk to you about composition and about theater. LeRoy Jenkins, a master string musician—he's concerned with opening up avenues for the violin and arriving at different approaches. He wants to utilize the whole instrument without having someone call him a 'classical' violinist.

"I myself was into mathematics and philosophy, seeing music from a mathematical perspective, and working with mathematical systems. I wanted to make up my own vocabulary, because I didn't want to follow anybody else. I wanted to find my own avenues. Now my music is a combination of all I learned in the AACM plus what I was working with in mathematics, in terms of sound relationships, densities, textures, different forms—what I call 'conceptual grafting,' which is about mixing different elements. I'm moving now toward trying to free the music in other ways, like playing in the streets, and bringing carpenters and automobile mechanics into the music. I'm starting to *see* the music, and to me the notion behind the music is just as important as the music itself. I can see how in the next ten years or so everybody will be able to bring something into the music from whatever their occupation is. Like, *you* bake cookies? *You* make ice cream? Well, we'll find a way we can create with *that*.

"I've just finished a piece for one hundred tubas. I'd like to go to all the high schools and get all the tuba players and have a parade and go down to City Hall playing this piece. I want to make music that is socially usable, and from which there can be direct results. Like, I dig watching shoemakers, watchmakers, ceramicists, work. I wish my art could be as useful as theirs is—I wish somebody could put tea or coffee in my music, or put their feet in it.

"But there are so many different types of music happening in the AACM. Chicago is a new center of the New Music. The atmosphere there seems to be more conducive to real creativity than New York. Nobody's famous there, and nobody's working, so if you're in music, it's only because you love it.

"Each person is realizing the different things he can do—his capacity for creating in different areas. This is something that's just beginning—we've been practicing and working for three or four years now, but it's still just beginning. What's happening now is really just a stepping stone and a way of people getting their minds together. The music has just begun. That's why the AACM is so important, because it's given us the opportunity to study exactly what's been opened up by people like Cecil Taylor, Ornette Coleman, John Coltrane, and 'classical' composers like John Cage—to find out what will be the disciplines that we will have to learn and what new avenues are available for the young musician to explore."

I asked Braxton to elaborate on the "classical" influences in his music.

"I want to be able to make use of everything that's in the air," he said. "I want to arrive at a *world* art that takes in everything. Nobody can tell me that John Cage, or David Tudor playing Stockhausen (which I just heard the other day, and which knocked me out), is not my music. There are a lot of people contributing in 'classical' music that I'm attracted to. I listen to 'classical' music an awful lot, and I'm very involved with it. Like, for me, John Cage is one of the two most important composers in the country today—the other is Duke

Ellington. Cage's knowledge and use of so many different concepts, textures, and properties have been a major contribution to music, and anybody who's in contemporary art has to know about them. Cage has done so much in terms of materials he's worked with and notions he's gone through—even the unsuccessful notions. And the fact that he's always trying to assimilate new concepts into the music, I find that very attractive.

"Of course, there are a lot of things Cage hasn't come to terms with. His music is almost all intellectual, all conceptual. He's so conceptual—like, the only way you can really deal with him is through some kind of intellectual system. That's true of Stockhausen too. Stockhausen (who is just the end of Webern) and Cage are like at the opposite poles of the same thing—Stockhausen with his empirical intellectualism, Cage with his metaphysical intellectualism. I met Cage once, and we talked about this. I was telling him that when you look in this life you see trees and rocks, but you also see people—people exist, egos exist (in the sense that each person is coming from his own head), and if that's true, then his music isn't really reflecting nature as much as he thinks it is, because people are just as much a part of nature as rocks and trees.

"I'm also aware that Cage has put down black art. But that's something I overlook, because that's something that *he* has to deal with, not me, and I devote my attention to the positive things he's contributed. Actually, I think Cage, in regard to jazz, is starting to listen now, and going through a period of change. He's been a victim of the scene, like everybody else; his inability to really expose himself to black art, to really be open to it and acknowledge it, has led him to a lot of wrong conclusions. But now I think he's becoming aware of the importance of black musicians, aware that he can learn from Cecil Taylor and Ornette Coleman. It's basically about improvisation. Nobody who walks into the next twenty years and calls himself a contemporary musician will be able to do it without having some understanding of what improvisation is all about in terms of the emotions behind it, the significance of it. Improvisation has been a property of world art—with the exception of Western art—for as long as this planet's been here. Most contemporary 'classical' musicians have now come to the junction where they're starting to understand that they're going to have to get into improvisation and that they're going to have to know about Duke and Miles. If you don't know about them, you're missing some essential knowledge, because they've been through it gloriously.

"But I'm saying that in spite of themselves and their emotional deficiencies, people like Cage and Stockhausen have done so much. One thing for sure, the next stage of creativity will employ the gains that Cage has made, as well as the gains that black art has made. That much is undeniable.

"Getting back to the music in the AACM," Braxton went on, "what's happening is that we're coming to realize that we have to bring all the different arts, all the different avenues, together. Music, painting, sculpting—they're all, in themselves, very limiting. We're working on getting to a wider spectrum with a label like 'art' or 'activity' or 'environment,' rather than 'music' or 'painting.' We want to incorporate as many different approaches and avenues as possible. We're working together in different kinds of groups, with different kinds of approaches. We have pieces where each musician plays ten balloons. I have a piece in which I conduct four chairs and four shovels; another piece where an audience comes, the musicians play three blocks away, then someone comes to tell you the concert is over. Leo Smith wrote a lot of 'plays' that we perform. All these different avenues are being covered.

"I mean, we can all play on changes, and most of us could read music in a symphony orchestra. But we're really not concerned with that anymore. Sometimes I do it because I like that kind of music. But it's not about proving anything anymore.

"What's happening now can be seen as a logical reaction to the lies this country was built on. But this is not so much a revolution as it is a final curtain being drawn on a particular period, and while the final curtain is being drawn, a curtain is opening on the next scene."

Although he was determined to stay in New York to "meet musicians, hear music, go to art galleries, and get into new avenues of expression," Braxton indicated that he had found the scene here particularly depressing.

"The musicians here are so divided economically, because people who control things divide them that way. But they're also divided from a lot of other standpoints, and the music in relation to the people is not as strong as it could be. There's so much dissension here. I feel like what's needed here is some kind of organizing by the artists along the lines of the AACM. In New York musicians are so separated. It would be nice if we could get together some kind of orchestra and take it to different neighborhoods. I mean, there are so many remarkable people walking around now creating music, whose music could reach out to all the people. But those in control won't let it get through to the public.

"There's been a conscious, plotted attempt to suppress and wipe out creative music in this country; I think you realize the significance of art in a culture and what the new art represents and who it threatens if people are able to hear it. It becomes a threat to existing values, because it can expand things and cause people to change the existing state of things. This is dangerous to people for whom change is not an advantage, so it becomes very . . . interesting.

"Let me tell you how deep this thing is. When our first record came out on Delmark, it was put down immediately. Immediately. And what was strange, the jazz cats said it wasn't jazz and the 'classical' cats said it wasn't 'classical' music. The critics said it wasn't even music. One way they'd put it down, they'd use comparison so as to try to destroy the morale within the group—compare me to Roscoe, compare LeRoy to someone —and they would say, well, the conclusion is that this cat's better than that cat. That's a very good way to destroy unity, and that is what was done. Everybody in the group knew it, but we were not in a position to do anything about it, like certain individuals—they know who they are—consciously exploited what we did and used it for something else."

Braxton moved to split. "You know," he paused to say, "here I've been talking all this time about art and artists, but actually I've never really wanted to fully identify with the idea of being an 'artist' or with the idea of playing music for a living. I'm afraid of being a 'musician' in the sense that society defines it—that is, of separating art from life, or of being in the music *business*. Art gets to be so manipulated. Like, *everybody's* a potential artist—butchers, bakers . . . I think the whole idea of art is something that Western culture has introduced so that it can be used on evil trips. Like, Western music was originally just a toy for rich people, something for the king to talk shit about. I feel that potentially we *all are the music*, our lives are art in the purest sense. So I don't want to sell my music anymore than I want to sell my hands. It's very evident, just checking out the scene, that if you tamper with the music and turn it into a synthetic, then in fact you turn *yourself* into a synthetic. It's very hard to participate and not have that happen.

"Of course, I can see how right now we need 'artists,' as such, to help show people that they're artists too, to show them what's meaningful. Consciousness is the most valuable thing that can be communicated right now—making people aware of themselves and their environment—and there has to be somebody holding the line and pointing out the options and the different avenues to learn about. In this country right now the people who are artists in the truest sense of the word are participating in activity which will bring this consciousness about. And then maybe we will be able to stop categorizing ourselves.

"Actually, some of the *most* creative people I've met are not involved in music. They are simply living what the music is about."

Rock & Regression: The Responsibility of the Artist

When we were conscious—when we saw precisely where it was, what we had to get to—what did we mean by "revolution"?

We meant that we wanted (and knew it was possible) to *turn the whole scene around*. We meant the construction of an environment which was free of preimposed standards, disciplines, and moralities, and conducive to the existential, and thus uncircumscribed, growth of all of our creative capabilities. We meant that we wanted to get to the most profound levels of who and what we are, and effect a revolution of *fundamentals*; of sensibility, of value systems, of the way we perceive and judge what is, and what is not, beautiful and real. We meant no less than the destruction of our "nature" and the resurrection of our Nature.

For many of us, rock, a phenomenon which embodied the energies and expressed some of the best perceptions generated by our awakening, and which was uniquely accessible to an enormous audience, gave promise of implementing the vision. Like the new "free" jazz, rock reflected a new and dynamic passion for life. "They wouldn't have this music at the White House," drummer Sunny Murray remarked to me in an interview. "If they did, they would all think they were being attacked. All of a sudden a rock or an avant-garde jazz musician jumps up and goes into his thing, and these people would run and hide under tables. . . . Now, if Lawrence Welk plays there—doo-pee-doo—oh, they cool now, man. *The submission in the music tells them that the people is submissioned.* But if a musician is playing like a rock or avant-garde jazz musician does, then, dig it, what's going on with the people?"

By the beginning of the 1970's, however, rock could claim about as much revolutionary potency as the Teamsters' Union.

A major factor in the decline of rock as a subversive energy has, of course, been the Aquarian-age businessman. But this agent of illusory revolution in the service of the status quo could not have been successful in rendering rock innocuous without the complicity of a fifth column, *i.e.*, a *susceptibility* within rock artists to the control and exploitation of their work. That susceptibility is not sufficiently explained by "ambition" or "avarice," per se. What is meant by "every man has his price" is that every man has his uncertainty about the validity and sanity of his perception of the truth. To "sell out" is to capitulate to that uncertainty.

It is uncertainty which ambushed rock's revolutionary thrust, and I think to look at certain simultaneous sociopolitical occurrences in the country in general may clarify what I mean.

If the notion of revolution is, for the majority of Americans, subconsciously very attractive and, in the absence of belief in themselves and in their infinite potentialities as human beings, an utterly untenable notion; and if the eruption of mutinous energies on all levels and in all departments of the culture in the last decade consequently produced so intolerable a havoc in the psyches of those Americans that, to repress those energies and restore "stability," they could elevate a Richard Nixon to the Presidency, a similar kind of conflict existed for rock artists in relationship to developments in their music.

Departing from old and familiar realities, rock musicians,

in the pursuit of a new reality, had first to negotiate the labyrinthine antechambers of that new reality. The difficult new complexities—self-conscious cerebrations, disjointed connections, etc.—which necessarily cropped up in their work as they sought to find entrance into that new reality, and which were embodied in "heavy" forms like "psychedelic" rock, created, for rock artists, not only confusions and opacities in their own perception of their work, but also threatened to lose them the support and encouragement of their audiences and to disconnect them from their audiences; *e.g.*, "We can't dance to rock anymore." When an artist, through recognition and acclaim, regains the love he lost when he announced that he was going to be an artist, the prospect that he will lose that love again by taking the next step and altering the content and style of his work presents an excruciating dilemma. I think that ordinary doubts which rock artists had about the sanity of their pursuit were exacerbated by these circumstances into unbelief. Disease, madness, and death, not the millennium, came to loom at the horizon. Rather than ride through the anxiety that grew out of this situation, and which, like the hysteria of the electorate, was an indication that they were moving from one reality to another, and symptomatic of growth, rock artists aborted the mission and retreated, in multiple ways, into a glib, deceptive radicalism, an Aquarian-passive reaffirmation of "simplicity" and the "basics": to wit, the Beatles' *Revolution, Get Back,* and *Let It Be*; the increasing pervasiveness, as encouraged by Bob Dylan and *Nashville Sky-line*, of country music—which music actually represents the quintessence of the pathological sensibility that has created necessity for a revolution—and the return to the songs and styles of 1950's rock and roll, a nascent stage of rock which belongs to a comparatively limited consciousness, a time when, say, street-gang kids were still battling *each other*, before they got hip to who the real enemy was.

(Similar regressive developments in the name of "love" and "communication," it has to be pointed out, have occurred in the musics of certain "New Thing" jazz musicians. The quasi-spiritualism which Pharaoh Sanders has settled for in albums like *Karma* and *Jewels of Thought*, and which, as one observer has remarked, has moved him dangerously close to Martin Denny, is the most glaring example. Albums like Ornette Coleman's *Friends and Neighbors* and Archie Shepp's *For Losers* are other examples. Still, I think, new jazz players have, by and large, done better at repelling the enemies within and without, and at sustaining the revolutionary integrity of their music, than have rock musicians, and I think this is because the black musician arrived at his present consciousness without the assistance of chemists or the local power company. He did not ascend via an air-conditioned express elevator, but up the stairs and through the ambush-ridden corridors of the stultifying superstructures which define our culture. The dangers he risked were far greater than a night at Bellevue. They involved his total being, the placing in jeopardy of his soul (of "soul"). And the natural, as opposed to artificial, or vicarious, quality of his trip has given him a certain conviction in the consciousness he has reached which makes that consciousness strong, dense, and certain, makes it less revocable and not so vulnerable to control, exploitation, and vitiation by the businessman, as is the consciousness of rock artists.)

But if it is a close to Herculean task for artists of revolutionary persuasion to keep their work alive and audacious in this society, it is also imperative. America writhes in malignancy, and artists (because it is their profession, their *raison d'être*, to be in touch with truths beyond the collective consciousness) constitute the only force that might affect remission and reversal. The artist (by definition) is supposed to be aware of, and in the pursuit of, an alternative to madness, and if he does not continue to pursue that alternative no matter how difficult social and personal circumstances may make such an endeavor he is an accomplice to his own destruction. But there are very few artists left who haven't succumbed, in one manner or another, to ambivalences within themselves which have weakened their resistance to the poisons in the air; poisons which have debilitated their energies, dimmed their passion, eroded their belief in the sureness and accuracy of their visions, disengaged their concentration and focus from where they knew the truth really was, and diminished their revolutionary ardor to, at best, a sexless reformism.

A recent, posthumous release of a Lenny Bruce record (*To Is a Preposition; Come Is a Verb*, on the Douglas label) has reminded me of an artist who provides a good example of what I mean. The actual demise of Lenny Bruce, who was cornered by the mad guardians of the pathological American sensibility into a terminal depression, was anticlimactic. Bruce entered death on the day he stood before the censorship court and, rather than remove his clothes, chose to ask the court for its "understanding." (There must have been a scent of the grave on Lenny's breath as he uttered that request.) Continually harassed in the last few years of his life by the police and the courts, Bruce was reduced to the level of his doubt. Too conflicted to say "fuck you" to his adversaries, and too hip to surrender completely, Bruce allowed himself to be seduced into the cul-de-sac of doing combat with American censorship laws *on the laws' terms*. Once he had done that, Bruce was no longer a figure of any serious consequence. He was into reform (which is to say, the liberalization and *perpetuation* of a murderous institution), not revolution. And he no longer had any place to take us that we had not already been.

(To be sure, one asks a great deal. Had Bruce told the court to fuck off, he may well have been assassinated. But there are deaths which open love and promise conception to the seed, and deaths which inspire nothing more than an onanistic tension and leave the seed to expire in the plumbing. Is it foolish to speculate that if Galileo had not renounced his discoveries in order to save his neck, we might have been blessed with the inspiration to put them to better use?)

But our vision was not reform, it was revolution. Indeed, when we were conscious, we were not talking about civilizing insanity. We wanted to *abolish* the police, not "humanize" them. Nor, when we were conscious, were we talking about hipping-up mediocrity or changing shallow mores and conventions, per se. Ad men and accountants smoking grass and growing hair. And we were not talking about saving malignant infrastructures and renovating superstructures. Like, we wanted to *eliminate* money, not spread it more equitably.

Ultimately the only revolutionary artists worthy of the name are those who can trust and accept what they see, and who are prepared to will their way through and past their misgivings and the various stages of their anxiety, the subtle and blatant ambushes of fever, pain, strain, illness, anger, depression, confusion, listlessness, that are the road signs and the cruel, but necessary, hazards of the trip. To do anything else is to become the lie they originally stood against and to create, at best, nothing more than another hip commodity. *Nashville Skyline* is a compromise, not an achievement—a withdrawal from anxiety, not a transcendence of it. It is the artist bringing it all back to the home which he did not, finally, have the courage to leave, and saying that, after all, the established order is correct.

Rock began as a visceral music, a body music, and, for sure, it must always be a music that calls the body to dance. But the dance must now have a *new* dynamic. And it must incorporate touch again. To *return* to simplicity—to the fox trot and lindy, which issued from an uptight emotional order whose cowardly puritanism eventually cornered us into the onanistic twist—is to deny and waste all that has been accomplished in the last decade. Rock must choose to pursue a *new* simplicity, a new reality *on the other side of anxiety,* which can be reached only by going *through* the anxiety that such an ambition engenders.

A *new* dance, a dance which belongs to a profoundly new sensibility, is what we meant.

[The foregoing article drew a letter from one Neil Connor (*Jazz & Pop,* September 1970), which asked me to clarify what I thought to be the "role of the artist in the revolutionary

project," and which went on to say: ". . . I would submit that
the revolutionary project can be most broadly defined as the
creation of new modes of existence on both the individual and
the collective level, and the integration of these modes of
existence into revolutionary community; that this creation/
integration must have as its primary aim the disintegration/
destruction of bourgeois modes of existence, and that all revolutionary activity can be discussed in the light of the process
of disintegration and integration—*i.e.*, in the light of the
totality. Rock and 'New Thing' jazz musicians and their music
are clearly important forces in the disintegration of bourgeois
culture, by virtue of their role in the liberation of the sub-
versive/sexual energies of the people. But it is becoming rarer
and rarer for the musicians to get to this point on the revolutionary path; they have almost never gone beyond it. The
chauvinism (to use a very overworked term) of the musicians
and their apparent desire to create pure art divorced from the
struggle of the people to secure liberated space and time for
their total liberation, seem to me the reasons for the impotence
of rock and new jazz music.

"What I am trying to say is that a large part of the uncertainty which causes the musicians to sell out is their failure
to identify themselves with the project of the transformation
of the totality of life—the lack of a real base from which to
launch their exploration and experimentation. Since they don't
belong to the revolution, they are the more easily used by the
reaction. Since they are not integrated into the revolution, they
are integrated into the reaction (the spectacular commodity
society, as the situationists call it). . . ."

My reply to Connor, also printed in the September 1970
issue of *Jazz & Pop*, follows. R.L.]

Neil Connor's definition of the "revolutionary project"
provokes no arguments from me. I disagree, however, with his
notion (in respect to the decline in revolutionary potency of
much of rock and the new jazz) that a "large part of the
uncertainty which causes . . . musicians to sell out [stems

from] their failure to identify themselves with the project of the transformation of the totality of life" and "their apparent desire to create pure art divorced from the struggle of the people to secure . . . liberation."

In the article to which Connor's letter is addressed, I implied that rock and the new jazz had equal significance in the revolutionary struggle, which I think, after a great deal of deliberation, is tantamount to lumping together Ché Guevara and the purveyors of bush-eois jackets as revolutionaries. Thus, in order to answer Connor's assertions, it is first of all necessary to acknowledge very basic and crucial differences between the qualities, goals, and functions of rock and those of the new jazz.

Quickly put (to do the subject justice would require a book), jazz is an art form, and rock is white popular music (a commodity form by definition), which makes any discussion of the rock artist "selling out," of hip capitalist exploitation of rock, or any judgment of rock's decline as a revolutionary force, academic. Rock's superiority over previous popular musical forms is simply the result of its existence in a period of expanded and heightened social, political, and psychological awareness, a period which makes possible and necessary a hip and relevant popular music. Continuing white popular music's traditional thievery from, and dilution of, black musical genius, and controlled at the very center of its aesthetic by economic considerations, rock's validity as a revolutionary agency (however seductive its unprecedented poeticism, high-energy, sociopolitical content, and blatant sexuality may make such a notion) is dubious to say the least. If an argument can be made for rock's service to the revolutionary project in its apparent provision of a means with which to popularize radical ideas, the fact that the process of popularization requires the diminution and corruption of those ideas subverts the service. For, once having been reduced to a blunted or twisted and relatively innocuous state, the ideas are employed as a wedge against their purest and most potent expressions. At best what is achieved by this circumstance is reform, not revolution; greater license, not real and total freedom (*e.g.*, the mythical "sexual revolution"); changes in the suprastructure, but not the infrastructure of the way we live (*e.g.*, the replacement of *Time* magazine by *Rolling Stone*). I am saying that the "revolution" which rock is supposed to represent is, if not entirely illusory, certainly modest.

A decline in boldness, in the last year or so, of many new jazz players is, I think, a much more meaningful subject to talk about.

The new jazz has heralded not merely a new style or, per se, a new way of making music, but a genuinely new *consciousness* and *sensibility*, and reaches in all of its implications and ramifications far beyond most prevailing revolutionary ambitions. Indeed, what the new jazz has gotten to, the emotional and spiritual truths at which it has arrived in, considering just one aspect, its collective improvisations, give hint (and I'm just touching here on a subject of great size and complexity) of a viable *anarchy*, *i.e.*, of a spiritually tuned way of living without externally imposed authority and order, which reveals even the "freedoms" of socialism as oppressive.

Connor acknowledges the "uncertainty" which has caused some new jazz musicians to "sell out" this vision, but I think his perception of the reasons behind that uncertainty are inaccurate. I think it has been the *failure of the people* to identify with the "transformation of the totality of life" implicitly announced in the properties, methods, and aesthetics of the new jazz which is to blame for the musicians' "uncertainty" and the consequent reduction in strength and audacity of their music.

Recognition being a principal source of validation, and validation being a principal source of energy and inspiration, it has been the resistance of audiences to the profound statement of the new jazz which is responsible for the enervation of the music. The absence of an audience has denied new-jazz musicians the mandate, as it were, to sustain and develop the more radical aspects of their music, and it has created in them pressing doubts as to the validity and sanity of their ideas. These doubts, and the basic necessity for a musician to have an audience, have compelled many new-jazz players to compromise their loftier visions and reduce the size and scope of their music.

The resistance of audiences, it should be noted, has been encouraged, perhaps decisively so, by the music scene's guardians of the status quo—publicity men who promulgate rock and maintain that jazz has "limited appeal," recording executives and concert promoters who, when they are not starving out the musicians, create neutralizing jazz-rock combinations, and writers who announce that jazz is dead. One ironic result of this situation is that anxieties which the new music caused in people who were not prepared to take a leap of the distance which it demanded have been cooled out by the receipt of "positive proof" that the musicians' most adventurous explorations were, even by revolutionary measure, too far out to make a viable music and, indeed, led them into a dead end from which they could only return.

As for the "role of the artist in the revolutionary project" (which Connor has asked me to define), I think, briefly, that it is not only to continue to chase, explore, and express emotional and spiritual truths which remain beyond the collective consciousness, but to find a way to sustain enough of a belief in them to try to live by them, and thus communicate their viability in the only way in which it is really possible to communicate such a thing, by example. Of course, the scene, as I have noted, does not make it easy to pursue such truths in the abstract, let alone to attempt their practical implementation. But I think the artist must endeavor to get to this place as fully as his psychic and economic circumstances will permit him to, because there is no other alternative.

Indeed, if the *artist* cannot summon the faith to assume that someday, in the not too distant future, the rest of us will hear his truths, and that those truths will wrest hegemony from the mercantile sensibility and inform and shape human society at its very foundations, then there is no point in any of us going on.

27450

781.5
S
Sinclair, John

Music & politics